Creating and Maintaining an Information Literacy Instruction Program in the Twenty-First Century

An ever-changing landscape

NANCY W. NOE

CP

CHANDOS
PUBLISHING

Oxford Cambridge New Delhi

Chandos Publishing
Hexagon House
Avenue 4
Station Lane
Witney
Oxford OX28 4BN
UK
Tel: +44 (0) 1993 848726
Email: info@chandospublishing.com
www.chandospublishing.com
www.chandospublishingonline.com

Chandos Publishing is an imprint of Woodhead Publishing Limited

Woodhead Publishing Limited
80 High Street
Sawston
Cambridge CB22 3HJ
UK
Tel: +44 (0) 1223 499140
Fax: +44 (0) 1223 832819
www.woodheadpublishing.com

First published in 2013

ISBN: 978-1-84334-705-7 (print)
ISBN: 978-1-78063-371-8 (online)
Library of Congress Control Number: 2013939100

British Library Cataloguing-in-Publication Data.
A catalogue record for this book is available from the British Library.

Typeset by Domex e-Data Pvt. Ltd., India
Printed in the UK and USA.

For

Ken and Jesse

Contents

List of figures and tables

Figures

Tables

Acknowledgements

I know of no other profession that is as willing to share expertise and support as is librarianship. I have been a librarian for over thirty years, working in public, corporate and academic libraries, and whatever successes I may have had, none could have been accomplished alone. I wish I could thank everyone who helped me along the way, but, alas, the pages would be voluminous. It is best that I thank those who have most recently joined me on this journey.

It is rare when one is able to consider co-workers as friends, yet I am indeed fortunate to be able to do just that. I want to thank my reference and instruction colleagues at Auburn University Libraries: Jaena Alabi, Barbara Bishop and her menagerie, Bob Buchanan, Marilyn Christianson, Tim Dodge, Claudine Jenda, Bridget Farrell, Adelia Grabowsky, Kasia Leousis, Greg Schmidt, Todd Shipman, Liza Weisbrod (we did it!) and Andy Wohrley. I appreciate their support, good natures and many kindnesses. I would also like to thank Paula Sullenger, Kim Connor, Pambanisha Whaley and the interlibrary loan staff, Helen Goldman, Aaron Trehub along with the systems staff, and Bob Yerkey – I do cause them a good bit of trouble from time to time.

I am also thankful to Toni Carter and Cate Calhoun of the instruction team. Toni's hard work and dedication to assessment have made our instruction program all the better. I do not know how we have managed heretofore without her rubber duckies and CATS. I appreciate Cate for her handling of all things FYE information literacy-related, both human and zombie.

It is good to have friends who walk with you along the way. Thanks to Kathy McClelland, Michelle Sidler, Alex Dyba and Jo Mackiewicz, who provided enjoyable lunch- and dinner-time companionship, as well as good and thoughtful guidance. Special thanks to Charles, Katherine and Anna Israel, with an extra special hug to John William. They helped Ken and me through a difficult time, and spending time with them reminds us of all that is good and right in the world.

My Dean, Bonnie MacEwan, is a model for all administrators. She too has provided guidance and support, and is always happy to share her experiences and advice to this still-learning librarian. Who else, when asked if it was okay to order 1500 hot dogs for a library open house, would say "Yes" without hesitation? Auburn University Libraries is led by the best, bar none.

I am thankful to Associate Dean for Public Services, Head of Reference and Instruction, Marcia Boosinger. Marcia advocated for my employment years ago, and then for my appointment as Instruction Coordinator during a time when it was difficult for her to do so. She is a mentor, friend and the best librarian and supervisor I have ever known. Her intelligence, dedication, integrity and genuineness inspire me every day.

I am also thankful to my long-time instruction team partner, Juliet Rumble. My dear and gentle philosopher friend always knows the right thing to say, listens when I need to vent, offers encouragement and support, and provides just the right counterbalance to this overly practical, stubborn Midwesterner. She takes good care of all the Noes, both near and far. When I first began this project, she encouraged me to "tell stories." I hope I have done her proud.

And, finally, I am so grateful to my family. My son, Jesse Benjamin Noe, is an absolutely amazing young man. I am so proud of his intelligence, warmth, humor, courage and adventurous spirit. I am also proud that he seems to have discovered a love and passion for teaching. No matter how many miles may separate us, he never, ever leaves my heart.

And then there is my husband, Kenneth William Noe, who after three decades remains the love of my life and my best friend. He provides unwavering love, support and chocolate; every day with him is a gift and blessing. That tree has got nothing on us, sweetheart! I look forward to years and years of watching chipmunks, birds and squirrels with him by my side, and wish for little else. He also makes a pretty fine in-house editor; however, I do not believe I have converted him into an in-text citation user. I promise to keep trying.

About the author

Nancy Noe currently serves as Instruction Coordinator at Auburn University Libraries, Alabama. Her research and scholarship centers on information literacy assessment and the integration of information literacy within the core, as well as the freshman-year experience. Nancy earned her MSLS degree at the University of Kentucky in 1983 and since then has held positions in public, corporate and academic libraries.

Introduction

Librarians have concerned themselves with helping users learn how to navigate and understand libraries and their resources for as long as libraries have existed. One imagines those responsible for early papyri repositories carefully instructing new apprentices and learned scholars on the care and treatment of scrolls, explaining how to locate the right record, providing handling instructions and wanting to teach the reader all there is to know about the document. I envisage them conducting these interactions with a certain sense of pride and a desire to convey the importance of the material. Of course, today's resources are not written on beaten reeds, but are digitized and read via LED screens. Users no longer have to travel to visit the great libraries; information is virtually accessible 24/7. Information is no longer measured in linear feet, but in gigabytes and terabytes. Nonetheless, librarians still want to help users access and understand information and information systems. We continue to do so with a sense of pride and professionalism.

When I first took on the role of instruction coordinator at a large research university, I immediately began reading seminal, helpful and inspiring works such as Curzon and Lampert's edited work, *Proven Strategies for Building an Information Literacy Program* (2007), Rockman's *Integrating Information Literacy into the Higher Education Curriculum* (2004), Gibson's work, *Student Engagement and Information Literacy* (2006), and Grassian and Kaplowitz's *Information*

Literacy Instruction: Theory and Practice (2009). In addition, every month I would read every article that pertained to library instruction and information literacy included in the latest editions of *College and Research Libraries* and *College and Research Libraries News* (CR&L News). I followed with interest discussions on the ILI-listserv (ACRL's instruction section's listserv), and tried to learn as much as I could. Despite the wealth of information available and a desire to learn, however, the time I had to devote to such academic and intellectual endeavors, while vitally important, soon gave way to an increased teaching load and additional day-to-day responsibilities. I needed a more practical, quick reference guide, a document to which I could turn to help remind me of what I needed to do. For me, this was the best practice guidelines, known formally as *Characteristics of Programs of Information Literacy that Illustrate Best Practices: A Guideline* (ACRL, 2012a). A group of faculty members, librarians, administrators and members of professional organizations developed the *Characteristics* over time, beginning in spring 2000. Subsequent drafts were revised, and the ACRL Executive Board approved the first edition during the summer of 2003. Five years later, members of the ACRL Information Literacy Practices Committee undertook a major revision and, in January 2012, the ACRL Executive Committee approved the latest edition. These guidelines "represent a metaset of elements" and are "not descriptive of any one program." They are "intended to help those who are interested in developing, assessing, and improving information literacy programs." In addition, "no program is expected to be exemplary with respect to all characteristics; [the] list is not prescriptive" (ibid.).

The *Characteristics* boil down best practices into categories, with detailed components provided as bulleted lists. Those bulleted lists kept me on track, while the overall document was one that I could take to supervisors and administrators as I discussed program planning and asked for support. It did, and still does, carry a great deal of weight; the authority of the ACRL combined with the "best practice" of the title has served me well over time.

However, they are guidelines ultimately, and not all programs will be able to achieve every element in every category. My home library's instruction program is a testament to that; it is still very much a work in progress. Yet whether you are just beginning to develop an information literacy instruction initiative, or are already directing an existing program, my hope is that this volume will serve as a useful guide to creating or reviewing a program as it expands upon categories and elements within the *Characteristics*. I will share some of my experiences and hopefully provide some "food for thought" as I augment the ACRL document. I truly enjoy my job as instruction coordinator and information literacy teacher; unequivocally it is the most rewarding and engaging position I have held in nearly thirty years as a professional librarian. Hopefully, my stories will add another layer of useful experience. Finally, I also hope that this book provides you the reader with practical and scalable examples, as well as with references to significant works that are worth exploring further.

Where are you now? Really?

Abstract: While many libraries today lay claim to having an information literacy instruction program, the reality of library instruction efforts may be somewhat removed from today's definition of "information literacy," as well as from the best practices in conducting a program. In order to determine whether or not one indeed has an information literacy program, an honest assessment from a number of stakeholders is required. In addition, in order to bring one's program into the twenty-first century, rebranding library instruction as information literacy instruction can only help to elevate the program, and align it with current practice, research and theory.

Key words: information literacy program, library instruction program, program assessment, program evaluation.

A reality check

Several years ago, my family and I spent five happy, fun-filled days at one of Florida's entertainment parks. Others seamlessly managed our accommodations, meals, transportation and entry to various attractions. Even the plane trip home appeared to be part of the enchanted experience. Reality, however, quickly greeted us at the gate as we emerged onto a busy concourse, found ourselves crammed on to a tram to baggage reclaim, and dealt with lost luggage. I much preferred the earlier state, living in the bubble of a perfect and carefree world. Human nature, being what it is, often allows us to escape easily into places of fantasy and illusion. In many cases those realms are pleasant indeed and they place little demand on our time and talents. But the real world always intrudes eventually.

Conducting a frank appraisal of one's own instruction program can prove equally difficult. Personally, I rather like to regard my program in the best light possible, and at times no doubt I ignore some basic realities. I do not believe I am alone in what some call "magical thinking." As I attend conferences, participate in workshops and collaborate with library colleagues both inside and outside of my institution, often I am struck by what I perceive to be an unrealistic perception of instruction and information literacy programs. While it may be as unsettling as walking into the lost-luggage office, facing the reality of one's instruction is the place to start.

The ACRL *Characteristics* are clear and definite; these are best *practices* for an "*Information Literacy*" program (ACRL, 2012a). Simply branding an instruction program as an information literacy program does not make it so. While one may list a definition of information literacy or detail the five ACRL standards on a web page, it is the performance or execution of practices which embody the core of those statements in meaningful and impactful ways that define and exemplify an information literacy program.

It is essential therefore that you can answer a critical question before you can build, or improve upon, your instruction: Do you truly have, or understand, what is required to build an information literacy program? Step back and make an honest, realistic and unbiased assessment of your programs. The following survey is a good starting point (see Figure 1.1).

Information literacy program survey

1. Course syllabi and class assignments are requested prior to each library session

   Always (3 points) Usually (2 points) Seldom (1 point)
   Never (0 point) _____

2. Library and teaching faculty meet to discuss and plan each library session

   Always (3 points) Usually (2 points) Seldom (1 point)
   Never (0 point) _____

3. The content of library sessions is based on ACRL information literacy standards

   Always (3 points) Usually (2 points) Seldom (1 point)
   Never (0 point) _____

4. Learning objectives/outcomes for each library session are obvious to both faculty and students

   Always (3 points) Usually (2 points) Seldom (1 point)
   Never (0 point) _____

5. Learning objectives/outcomes for each library session are based on ACRL performance indicators and student outcomes

   Always (3 points) Usually (2 points) Seldom (1 point)
   Never (0 point) _____

6. Library sessions are tailored around a specific class assignment

   Always (3 points) Usually (2 points) Seldom (1 point)
   Never (0 point) _____

7. Library sessions are led by librarians who make use of "guide on the side" pedagogy as opposed to "sage on the stage" pedagogy

   Always (3 points) Usually (2 points) Seldom (1 point)
   Never (0 point) _____

(continued)

3

8. Library sessions make use of pedagogies that meet different student learning styles

   Always (3 points) Usually (2 points) Seldom (1 point) Never (0 point) _____

9. Physical facilities for library sessions (classrooms/ computer labs) are adequate

   Always (3 points) Usually (2 points) Seldom (1 point) Never (0 point) _____

10. Library administration provides support for an adequate number of teaching personnel to meet instruction needs

    Always (3 points) Usually (2 points) Seldom (1 point) Never (0 point) _____

11. Library administration provides library instructors with training and development opportunities

    Always (3 points) Usually (2 points) Seldom (1 point) Never (0 point) _____

12. Instructional support materials are based on specific information literacy outcomes and are focused on process (as opposed to handouts and web pages which are comprised of inventory lists or links to resources)

    Always (3 points) Usually (2 points) Seldom (1 point) Never (0 point) _____

13. Librarians include student learning assessment(s) in each library session

    Always (3 points) Usually (2 points) Seldom (1 point) Never (0 point) _____

14. Librarians have time in their schedule to create new classes and develop new pedagogies

    Always (3 points) Usually (2 points) Seldom (1 point) Never (0 point) _____

15. Librarians make use of "active learning" in library sessions

    Always (3 points) Usually (2 points) Seldom (1 point)
    Never (0 point) _____

16. Students are engaged in library sessions and are allowed to provide examples for demonstration and discussion

    Always (3 points) Usually (2 points) Seldom (1 point)
    Never (0 point) _____

17. Students are allowed time in library sessions to practice what was learned and to ask questions

    Always (3 points) Usually (2 points) Seldom (1 point)
    Never (0 point) _____

18. Faculty and library instructors meet to reflect on library sessions in order to improve subsequent sessions

    Always (3 points) Usually (2 points) Seldom (1 point)
    Never (0 point) _____

19. Library sessions are well integrated (and articulated) within specific curricula

    Always (3 points) Usually (2 points) Seldom (1 point)
    Never (0 point) _____

20. Faculty are aware of "information literacy" and their role, and the library's role, in information literacy

    Always (3 points) Usually (2 points) Seldom (1 point)
    Never (0 point) _____

    Total points _____

Figure 1.1 Information literacy instruction program survey

If you scored:

1–20 points

It would be difficult to consider this program an information literacy program. While the program may be offering and teaching a number of library sessions, the score suggests that the most basic elements for information literacy are not present. This indicates a challenging, yet not insurmountable, road ahead. Consider your score an opportunity for substantive growth and an opportunity to build a program based on best practice.

21–30 points

The evidence suggests an information literacy program in its earliest stages. Substantial effort will be required to develop it further; the prospects for shaping the program on best practice and theory should serve as a motivating factor.

31–45 points

This program's librarians have implemented a core of best practices for an information literacy program. The score suggests it may be time for a program review, which will provide opportunities to enhance the current program and implement new practices to move the program forward.

46–60 points

This program demonstrates a majority of the best practice measures for an information literacy program. Such programs serve as examples for other programs and those involved in the program should share their expertise with others.

Real assessment requires more than self-assessment, of course. To ensure that your scoring is accurate, ask other stakeholders – such as library colleagues, library administrators and faculty who bring classes for sessions – to complete the scale. If their ratings are roughly the same, the consensus would suggest that the score provides a realistic view of your program. If the ratings among various stakeholders do not correspond, however, then you need to consider the possibility that there is a true disconnect between how you see your program and how others see it. As uncomfortable an idea as it may be, it is essential at this point to assume that how others perceive your program may be the more accurate and authentic representation. Consider meeting with those surveyed to solicit additional clarification and feedback. In making additional inquiries, remain positive and ask for responses predicated upon the promise that the information will be used to improve the program; do not be defensive or to use the opportunity to "set them straight." Our stakeholders may be holding up the very mirror needed to reflect the real nature the program.

Unified language, unified mission, unified program

Now ask another question: What do you call your program? According to a study of multicultural, multilingual organizations, the adaptation and consistent use of common language improves group cohesion and increases the frequency of communication (i.e., the number of personal interactions) (Lauring and Selmer, 2010). Common language usage, including simplified and controlled vocabularies, allows for communication to pass more quickly and accurately. As a result, shared language works to "improve the clarity of communication among professionals in the same line of work" (Thrush, 2001: 290). Librarians are well versed in controlled vocabularies and conventional thesauri, yet when it comes to nomenclature regarding instruction and information literacy, we may not be modeling librarianship's best practice.

Currently, I serve as Coordinator of Instruction at a level one research land-grant university based in the southeastern United States. Largely a residential campus, our student body stands at roughly 25 000 students: 21 000 undergraduates and 4000 graduate students. In addition to a strong general liberal arts and science curriculum, program offerings include engineering, nursing, agriculture, pharmacy, education, architecture, veterinary medicine and business. Degrees awarded range from certificates to doctorates.

Our library is a member of the Association of Research Libraries and the Association of Southeastern Research Libraries. There is one main library and two smaller branch libraries (architecture and veterinary medicine). In addition to holding more than 3.5 million volumes, the main library supports a learning commons and a study commons, and partners with the university's writing center, its peer-to-peer tutoring center, information technology, and student advising. The library is a hub of student learning and activity, and last year's annual door count registered nearly 1.7 million visits, with 2 million virtual visits to the library's homepage. The library's workforce is comprised of 30 library faculty, 45 staff members and a number of student workers.

Our information literacy program is robust and nearly 700 face-to-face instruction classes are taught annually. The majority of these classes are conducted by library faculty (14 members) within the Reference and Instruction Department. As instruction coordinator, I lead a team of three library faculty whose main appointment is weighted to instruction, and the four of us teach a large number of first-year and core classes. Other library teaching faculty also teach a number of core classes in addition to their subject-level instruction.

We have three computer instruction labs within the library; each designated within the online scheduler by abbreviated name and location. The third-floor lab is the

3rd floor BI lab. Two labs are located on the second floor, the 2nd floor lobby lab (aptly named as it is adjacent to our front entrance lobby) and the 2nd floor BI lab (the placard outside the door says "Bibliographic instruction," no doubt put in place when the space was first designated as library instruction space). During the fall and spring semesters, student circulation workers prepare the labs each day for teaching. Student workers look at the master scheduler and if a class is being held in any particular lab they log on the computer terminals, test the instructor station and generally prepare the room for a day of teaching. The technical configuration for each lab is a little different and, as I was conducting training one day, a student mentioned she was looking forward to learning how to set up the "bi-lab." The student pronounced this "bi-" as in bifold, bi-level or bilingual, not "B" "I." I asked why she called it that. She replied that she used that terminology because the lab served two (dual) purposes. When classes are over for the day, we open our labs for student use. In her mind, the lab was used in two very different ways, and hence the "bi-" moniker made perfect sense to her. "BI" or "bibliographic instruction" were foreign concepts to this bright student. She did not speak librarian-ese.

Worse, our language has too many dialects. As librarians, we tend to call our programs by the names that were used to describe library instruction while receiving library degrees. In my own experience, in the mid-1980s, "bibliographic instruction" was the correct and proper term. "User education" became popular shortly afterwards. By the early 1990s, "information literacy" had been adopted by the profession. Language is important and can be internalized to the point that it is difficult to change. Even our Library of Congress subject headings provide little clarity (see the box on p. 10).

Bibliographic Instruction

USE   Library Orientation (LoCSH 817)

Library Orientation

Used for   Bibliographic instruction

Libraries and readers – programmed instruction [former heading]

Library instruction

Library research – study and teaching

Library user orientation

Orientation (library use) (LoCSH 4548)

User Education (Information Science)

USE   Information Services – User Education (LoCSH 837)

Information Literacy

Used for   Literacy, information

Related term   Information science

Narrower term   Electronic information resource library

Internet literacy

Media literacy (LoCSH 3851)

Language can also become institutionalized, and once set in personal and organizational convention it becomes intractable. Curious about the frequency of use, I conducted a search using the more familiar terms within professional databases and Google Scholar. What I discovered was a veritable babel of local vocabularies (see Table 1.1).

Table 1.1 Frequency of use comparison

Search terms	Number of results		Google Scholar	
	ERIC Information Science & Technology Abstracts (LISA) Library Literature and Information Science Index (Wilson) Academic Search Premier Without date limiter	ERIC Information Science & Technology Abstracts (LISA) Library Literature and Information Science Index (Wilson) Academic Search Premier Date limiter: 2002–2012	Without date limiter	Google Scholar Date limiter: 2002–2012
"information literacy"	13 434	10 777	59 500	21 600
"library instruction"	9 914	3 326	18 100	9 680
"user education"	1 768	684	14 900*	8 050*
"bibliographic instruction"	8 885	3 644	8 830	3 840

Note: * Within Google Scholar, the majority of results for "user education" were not associated with libraries or library instruction.

This rudimentary analysis seems to suggest that "information literacy" now has precedence, and has had for the past decade. The following chapter deals in part with *defining* information literacy, but for now let us simply consider nomenclature. Perhaps it is time for librarians to commit to the use and benefits of a common, shared language. If we as a profession continue to debate and change what we call our programs, then how can we expect our users to understand and participate in shared missions and goals? As challenging as it may be for some institutions – and realizing that personal and professional arguments for other names and terminology have their local merits – the term "information literacy" is simply the fundamental core of an "information literacy instruction" program. While it may be a comfortable habit to call our program by an old, familiar name, it is time to stop using "user education" and "bibliographic instruction." Such terms may be shorthand for those deeply rooted in the profession, but they confuse those who are not as well versed in the professional jargon of an MLS degree program, and they directly impact effectiveness and success. As professionals, we must strive to be more diligent, deliberate and consistent with language and word choices. Language can – and does – change. Students no longer ask for help in making a "Xerox;" instead they ask to make copies, or, even more recently, they ask for assistance in "scanning" or "digitizing" articles. And so we need to take down the "Bibliographic instruction" signs.

Of course, there are barriers. At one of my previous institutions I was *the* librarian, and I managed reference, circulation, cataloging and instruction by myself. Likewise, many of us wear several different hats and hold responsibilities in addition to instruction. Colleagues who may also participate in teaching might have a myriad of other duties. In addition, many of us are under a great deal of pressure from library administration and campus administration to create model programs, usually without proper support or even understanding of the resources and time required. Few librarians work at an institution that provides all of the support needed to create and maintain a fully formed, fully functioning program which meets all of the best characteristics.

The goal then must be to move forward, and to not let obstacles, whether real or perceived, stop or hinder program growth and success. Each of the subsequent chapters outlines a category of best practice. The *Characteristics* are explicit:

> The characteristics identify and describe features notable in information literacy programs of excellence. The characteristics are not, however, descriptive of any one program, but rather represent a metaset of elements identified through examination of many programs and philosophies …
>
> The characteristics are primarily intended to help those who are interested in developing, assessing and improving information literacy programs.
>
> … no program is expected to be exemplary with respect to all characteristics; this list is not prescriptive. Rather, individuals are encouraged to consider their library and institutional contexts in establishing information literacy program goals and strategies while incorporating these characteristics.
>
> (ACRL, 2012a)

To assist in moving an information literacy program forward, allow best practices to serve as a road map. Not all programs have the same destination; not all programs need to incorporate each and every characteristic. One size does not, and should not, fit all. Scale the characteristics to best meet your user, library and institutional needs while sloughing off magical thinking.

2

Why are we here and where do we want to go? Program mission, goals and objectives

Abstract: In order to provide guidance and direction for an information literacy instruction program, the development of a well-articulated program mission statement, with goals and objectives, serves as a clear road map for all constituents. In addition, by formulating and situating written guidelines on and within strategic campus documents, the program's importance and value are enhanced within the institution.

Key words: mission statement, goals, objectives, planning, institutional value.

Introduction

One of my earliest missteps in leading an instruction program was ignoring the importance of systematic, organized and documented planning. While I had vague notions of the program's requirements and the direction in which it needed to go, it would have helped my colleagues, supervisors, collaborators and students if I had articulated a strategic plan for all to examine. There is a program destination, but, unlike speaking into the GPS of a mobile phone and having the phone respond with each and every turn, or again placing a beginning and end location address into an online mapping system, the details of the journey in between must be provided by those directing the program. They are not automatic.

Developing a mission statement

A mission statement is a "simple, clear, and compelling statement that focuses on the most important thing you want people to know" (Wallace, 2004: 6). An instruction program's mission statement is much like the concluding destination, setting the direction for the journey. It should not be viewed as a pro forma, static and uninspiring fragment of verbiage, but rather as a dynamic document. It should motivate the reader – whether a faculty member, staff member, student, librarian or administrator – to "want to relate to it and want to work toward attaining the goals embodied by it" (Grassian and Kaplowitz, 2005: 9).

What, then, are the components a program mission statement? According to the *Characteristics* the following elements should be included.

Defining your subject

Your mission statement must include a definition of information literacy and be consistent with the ACRL Information Literacy Competency Standards for Higher Education (ACRL, 2012a).

When it comes to defining information literacy, I adhere to the sentiment expressed in the title of Owusu-Ansah's article "Debating definitions of information literacy: enough is enough!" (2005). He makes a convincing case that the

ACRL definition works for most, and that continued debate on the issue of "appropriate definitions and descriptors ... promises no practical benefits." Owusu-Ansah adds that, "Such activities can ... become an unfortunate drain on precious time and energy. That time and energy could be more meaningfully spent on actually working to improve student capabilities, on exploring the role the library can play in that process, and on determining the legitimacy and desired extent of the library's participation in the education of information literate students" (ibid.: 373).

Certainly, there is an ongoing dialog within the profession on this topic, and discussions can motivate readers to consider future options and trends. Narratives making the case for digital literacies, visual literacies, multi-modal literacies (Jewitt, 2006) and meta-literacies (Mackey and Jacobson, 2011) are important philosophical and intellectual discussions and certainly point to areas the profession needs to address as we integrate technologies and learning. What librarians risk, however, is being caught up in the arguments of naming convention and theory; arguments that may never end with a clear consensus. How willing are those leading programs to decide on a model and path that may not be sustainable or viable in the foreseeable future? Often, our constituents find even the most basic understanding of information literacy challenging, and to bandy about differing terms, definitions and theories can only serve to confuse users, and perhaps even ourselves. For the time being, however, Campbell makes a strong case that the ACRL definition is undeniably "broad enough to encompass the entire spectrum of information skills ... and will probably still be applicable for many decades" (Campbell, 2004: 4). As the program mission statement must place information literacy at the program's core, as well as indicate a commitment to that purpose (Zmuda, 2007: 24), the ACRL standard definition accomplishes the objective. It reads:

> To be information literate, a person must be able to recognize when information is needed, and have the ability to locate, evaluate and use effectively the needed information.
>
> (ACRL, 2000: 2)

As in the previous chapter's discussion on using shared vocabulary in labeling a program, librarians also must come to a consensus on using a unified definition; the program mission statement must reference the five ACRL information literacy standards as well. Our professional standards are well-established, practical and well-articulated.

To be information literate one must be able to:

- determine the extent of information needed;
- access the needed information effectively and efficiently;
- evaluate information and its sources critically;
- incorporate selected information into one's knowledge base and use information effectively to accomplish a specific purpose; and
- understand the economic, legal and social issues surrounding the use of information, and access and use information ethically and legally.

(Ibid.: 2–3)

Aligning the mission statement with the mission

Your mission statement must align with the library's overall mission (ACRL, 2012a).

To begin to align a program's mission statement with the library's mission, you should collect and compare all relevant documents, including the library's mission and/or vision statements, the library's goals and objectives and its strategic plans (Cottrell, 2011: 517). Analyze the documents and scan for advantageous language. Rarely will there be an exact word match for information literacy, yet words and phrases whose meanings exemplify or represent an aspect of an information literacy program will be present. Many library mission statements, for example, are likely to use phrases such as "educational mission," "educational support," "student success," "learning support," and "academic support." These phrases can be parlayed into support for an instruction program.

Not all libraries have mission statements, of course. Others may be dated and may not reflect current trends and practices. Look for opportunities to introduce or refine mission statements in these cases. One of the most powerful motivators for any institution is regional accreditation (Hardesty, 2007: 17–18). Accreditation serves as an authoritative influence for strategic documentation and planning, as well as assessment, which will be discussed in more detail in Chapter 10. In addition to accreditation, other opportunities to introduce or refine library and program mission statements include the addition of new curricula, internal curriculum and program reviews and campus expansions. Use whatever openings available to initiate mission statement inclusion.

For example, as the lone librarian at a technical college, I once was tasked with writing the library's mission statement in preparation for an accreditation visit. I crafted what I considered to be a well-written, descriptive and inclusive draft. I forwarded the statement to my supervisor, who decided to form a team for review. This administrator, along with another campus official and I, began work on the revision.

At our initial meeting, my two colleagues agreed that the draft needed to be "fixed." At the next meeting, my immediate supervisor had edited the original statement into a single, twelve-word statement. The other administrator had taken the time and energy to draft a five-page mission statement! Needless to say, that meeting desolved quickly into a power struggle between the two, and subsequent meetings were just as unproductive. To this day, I still have the haunting recollection of a twenty-minute debate over the use of a single preposition. Obviously, this exercise was not effective, and I suggested that we take a break from the drafting process and use the time to contemplate the work we had managed to accomplish. While some might consider this an act of subterfuge, I considered it to be a necessary tactic and after a few short weeks, the administrators had moved on to other projects. When the time came for the library to report for the accreditation self-study, I inserted my original work without opposition.

In writing an overall mission statement or a program statement, there are those who suggest that the optimal approach is to work in teams. Best practice theory does indicate that collaborative efforts tend to maximize results. As in my experience, however, if the structure of the team, or other factors, conspire against drafting a useful statement, sole authorship is a viable option.

Consistency is key

Your mission statement must adhere to the format of campus strategic documents and appear in appropriate institutional documents (ACRL, 2012a).

Campus strategic documents include the college or university mission statement, strategic plans, annual reports, program and curriculum review documents, campus-wide initiative plans (e.g., writing across the curriculum) and white papers. Use these as guides; model the language and mimic the format. Once a program mission statement is developed, advocate its inclusion in as many library and campus documents as possible (Corrall, 2008). In addition to the documents cited above, integrate the mission statement into library web pages, library strategic documents, instructional web pages and instructional brochures or newsletters to maximize exposure and embed the program prominently within the library and institutional environment.

Defining your audience

Your mission statement must include campus stakeholders and reflect their contributions and expected benefits (ACRL, 2012a).

This aspect of a mission statement answers the "who" question. While a noble cause, an information literacy program cannot meet the needs of "everyone," and to articulate a program that will do so will only lead to failure. As a rule of thumb, an instruction program's primary audience should be limited to the students, faculty and staff of an institution. This does not mean that all who cross the library threshold – either physically or virtually – will not benefit from information literacy constructs. It does signify, however, that the lion's share of programming and effort will be focused on a core and central audience. It is this primary effort that will also be the focus of resource allocation and assessment.

Defining your purpose

Your mission statement must promote lifelong learning and professional development (ACRL, 2012a).

An information literacy instruction program helps students learn the skills necessary for academic success, but its impact should not stop at graduation. We are also preparing students for professional and personal success. While information literacy has been a fundamental concept within education for decades, the workplace, less familiar with the nomenclature of our profession, nonetheless recognizes the same skill components (Leavitt, 2011; Lloyd, 2011). In an investigative study among various professionals, the following practices were identified as information literacy experiences:

- using information technology for information awareness and communication;
- finding information from appropriate sources;
- executing a process;
- controlling information;
- building a personal knowledge base in a new area of interest;
- working with knowledge and personal perspectives adopted in such a way that novel insights are gained; and
- using information widely for the benefit of others.

(Bruce, 1999)

Similarly, in a survey of corporate managers conducted by James Madison University (JMU) Library in collaboration with JMU's College of Business, when asked about necessary research and information skills for entry-level workers, participants cited "the ability to synthesize, summarize, and present information; the ability to perform data analysis; and the ability to think critically and creatively about research topics and findings" (Sokoloff, 2012: 11).

Librarians must consider workforce development. Here's an example. I teach a number of general English composition classes. While the composition curriculum has moved well beyond the traditional literature intensive focus, a few instructors still want library classes to focus solely on a particular subject-specific database or narrow literature topic. The argument I use when planning information literacy outcomes for those classes is that we, for the most part, are not training future academicians, but career professionals: accountants, nurses, engineers and a variety of other professionals. They are going to become the professionals we will rely on for our health, our bridges or our audit-free tax returns. One of the main objectives of a library session should be to help students learn to access, evaluate and select credible and reliable resources; practices we hope continue as they make information choices within the workplace.

Information needs also permeate everyday life. For example, the number of adult users who are turning to the Internet to access health information is growing (Fox and Jones, 2009). While health educators are contending with web-based health information needs in clinical settings (Wright and Grabowsky, 2011), in working with patients they are also building upon and reiterating the same kind of selection and evaluation strategies students may have learned as they worked on their first research paper. Any number of social interactions require citizens to be information savvy. For example, the voting public, bombarded with print and visual political rhetoric, must be able to navigate the onslaught of candidates' promotional materials and make an informed decision during an election. Parents may need to research and evaluate area school systems. Consumers should research and evaluate purchases, such as appliances and automobiles. Even something like purchasing a daily cup of coffee could entail looking at nutritional values and making a decision based on a calorie count. It is difficult to find an example of information not being a part of daily life.

There is a multitude of library mission and instruction program statements available on the web. Here are three which exemplify best practice:

Library Instruction Mission Statement – Hunter College

The Library Instruction Program serves the students, faculty and staff of Hunter College. The purpose of the Program is to assist members of the college community with developing information-seeking abilities appropriate for their individual levels of scholarship and to support their research. Through this program, the library facilitates access to the vast resources available to the College, fosters a sense of independence and responsibility and encourages a collaborative relationship with Reference/Instruction faculty. The classroom faculty is invited to work with library instruction faculty in designing course-related assignments that include information literacy objectives. The Library Instruction Program incorporates teaching strategies and methodologies that respond to individual differences in learning including level, style and culture.

Source: http://library.hunter.cuny.edu/services/information literacymission, accessed 5 August 2012.

Information Literacy Mission – University of North Carolina at Pembroke

As part of the mission of the University of North Carolina at Pembroke, the Mary Livermore Library plays a critical role in supporting the university's commitment to academic excellence. As such, the Library's Instructional Services area promotes information literacy through a formal instruction

---

program that aims to provide the university's campus community with the skills needed to find, retrieve, analyze and use information. Instructional Services offers students, faculty and staff a structured approach towards learning information literacy skills that is hands-on and curriculum based.

Source: http://www.uncp.edu/tlc/sacs/SACS_Report/submission/ documents/1144.pdf, accessed 5 August 2012.

San Jose State University Library – Our Instructional Program – Mission

The campus Library and Information Literacy Instruction Program collaborates with faculty, instructional staff and campus administrators to pursue its primary mission: to make information literacy integral to the SJSU experience through curriculum-focused instruction, provision of instructional materials and faculty–librarian cooperation. We work with you to ensure that students in on-campus, hybrid and distance courses and programs develop the skills, attitudes and knowledge that they need in order to become efficient, effective users and producers of information. This essential set of abilities will not only give students some of the critical tools necessary for success in their academic careers at the university, but also help them prepare for a lifetime of learning.

Source: https://library.sjsu.edu/instructional-services/our-instructional-program, accessed 5 August 2012.

Goals and objectives

Now that you have developed an information literacy program mission statement you will need to generate goals and objectives in support of that mission. As with the development of your mission statement, these must be consistent with the library's overall mission as well as the home institution's mission. Goals and objectives are not the same thing. Goals are the "concrete and specific means for ... implementing the mission" (Hayes, 1993: 50) and they "provide a framework that guides subsequent action" (Hensley, 2004: 3). In contrast, objectives "will measure [its] progress toward reaching a goal" (Nelson, 2001: 79). Include a time frame for completion (ibid.: 86). Think of it this way, if the mission statement is the end point of your journey, goals are the daily milestones, with objectives being the actual roads, turns and stops along the way. Goals are broad, general intentions. Objectives are the steps taken to reach a goal, and they are distinct and tangible.

The number of goals and objectives set for an information literacy program must be such that the majority can be accomplished. Remember, you will be reviewing the success of each goal and objective so, truly, the "fewer goals and outcomes the better" (ibid.: 82). In addition, the *Characteristics* (ACRL, 2012a) suggest that the following also be included:

- accommodate input from institutional stakeholders;
- clearly present the integration of information literacy across the curriculum for students' academic pursuits and effective lifelong learning (see articulation);
- accommodate the sequential growth of students' skills and understanding throughout their education; and
- take into account all learners served by or connected to the institution regardless of delivery systems or location.

Here is a good example from the University of Washington's University Libraries Student Learning Goals:

Learning goal 1: University Libraries fosters critical inquiry and thinking skills in students.

Critical thinking encompasses problem solving, decision making, reflective thinking, ethical reasoning and the ability to question one's assumptions when evaluating evidence and arguments. Students who think critically acquire skills and familiarity with modes of inquiry and examination from diverse disciplinary perspectives, enabling them to access, interpret, analyze and synthesize information.

Student learning outcomes associated with critical inquiry:

1. Student identifies and evaluates new and prior information relevant to a research topic in order to contextualize research questions or problems.
2. Student uses a variety of strategies and research finding tools (article databases, e-journals, catalogs, data sets, and more) in order to identify and use sources most appropriate to the research question or problem.
3. Student uses multiple forms of evidence gathered from various sources and evaluates the credibility and accuracy of each source in order to support research goals.
4. Student uses information across multiple formats (print, visual, multimedia, data, etc.) and genres in order to seek and evaluate relevant or appropriate evidence.
5. Student applies ethical and legal principles when accessing and using information sources from all formats and contexts.

Learning goal 2: University Libraries supports students in the creation of new knowledge and contributions to the greater scholarly and research community.

The creation and dissemination of new knowledge leads to sharing new understandings, solutions and perspectives in a purposeful and ethical way. Students who produce new knowledge acquire the skills needed to make effective use

(continued)

27

of multiple information sources and to participate in the collaborative production of intellectual property.

Student learning outcomes associated with knowledge production:

1. Student demonstrates awareness of discourses across academic disciplines, communities and professions, including how each produces, contextualizes and disseminates information.
2. Student synthesizes existing information and applies it to new settings and complex problems in order to generate new topics, hypotheses or solutions.
3. Student effectively interacts and publishes with peers, experts or others in order to collaboratively produce knowledge for various audiences and in various media.
4. Student uses appropriate tools, technologies and strategies in order to organize, integrate and present information effectively.
5. Student demonstrates understanding of copyright and citation conventions in order to meet the ethical and legal responsibilities required when creating intellectual property.

Source: http://www.lib.washington.edu/teaching/university-libraries-student-learning-goals-and-outcomes, accessed 8 August 2012.

Conclusion

Once all the components are in place, it is time to pull everything together and publish in a visible, accessible way. The use of web pages, wikis and LibGuides allows for this task to be accomplished quickly and easily. A main information literacy web page can link to any number of other supporting web pages and documents. A one-stop, or first stop, if you will, for your entire information literacy program.

3

Planning. Yes, more planning

Abstract: Program assessment is vital to the planning process. A number of evaluations – including SWOT analysis, needs assessment, environmental scans and focus groups – may be employed to help analyze a program's strengths and weaknesses, and identify areas for growth and improvement.

Key words: planning, SWOT analysis, needs assessment, environmental scan, focus groups.

Program assessment

The mission statement, goals and objectives created serve as the crucial starting point, of course, and their distinct purpose is to provide "an essential foundation for successful strategic planning for the future" (Balas, 2007: 32). According to the *Characteristics*, planning for an information literacy program "articulates and develops mechanisms to implement and/or adapt components" for the plan, and points to the evidence necessary to help shape the blueprint and plan strategically (Harley et al., 2006). The plan requires even more detail, however, and it is time to do some research for the journey, part of which includes gathering data. Librarians love to collect data: gate counts, circulation statistics, web hits and database usage are among just a few of the profession's favorite metrics. Collecting data for instruction program planning is merely an extension of that data collection (Koontz, 2006: 1).

A SWOT approach

So, how to proceed? In Chapter 1, I discussed making a candid assessment of your overall information literacy program. To continue this evaluation, the *Characteristics* propose the following strategies. The first is to "address current opportunities and challenges" (ACRL, 2012a). One of the best and most widely-recognized ways to accomplish this is by using the business-modeled acronym, SWOT (Strengths, Weaknesses, Opportunities, Threats) (Dictionary of Business, 2002: 496).

Consider analyzing the following aspects for a SWOT analysis:

- library culture
- administrative support
- depth of human resources
- experience/knowledge of staff
- the use of technology
- perceptions and reactions to innovation and creativity
- the customer service model
- the quality of an existing program
- costs and benefits
- reputation
- stakeholders, and
- marketing and communication opportunities.

Much like the instruction program vs. information literacy program, it is best for the SWOT assessment to be conducted by more than one individual. A small team, usually of at least five people, is the norm (Simoneaux and Stroud, 2011). Note that by asking others to participate in a program's SWOT exercise, one also meets the characteristic of "librarian, faculty and administrator collaboration" at the outset.

A SWOT report need not be lengthy. A single-page, bulleted outline should include the most relevant and critical findings. Consider the following example, which was recently completed by the instruction team at my library in preparation for the development of a new overall five-year strategic plan:

Strengths

- Well-established partnership with English Composition general education class; library sessions required, information literacy learning outcomes integrated into curriculum and phased with assignments.
- Core group of dedicated, interested and responsible teaching librarians.
- Supportive mid- and upper-level administration.
- Good physical space (two computer teaching labs with current technology).
- Initiation of campus-wide information literacy assessment.
- Library instruction faculty representation on campus core curriculum oversight committee.
- Library instruction faculty representation on campus teaching effectiveness committee.

Weaknesses

- Too many classes; not enough teaching faculty.
- Lack of mission statement specifically for instruction.

(continued)

31

- Lack of comprehensive documentation for instruction program.
- A minority number of library teaching faculty who require in-depth teaching development.
- Resistance to assessment.
- Resistance to incorporating active learning into classroom instruction.

Opportunities

- Opportunity to grow information literacy program via upper-level major courses.
- Continued opportunities for collaboration.
- Continued opportunities for teacher training and development.
- Development of upper-level information literacy instruction courses in conjunction with new university writing initiative.
- Possibility for additional instruction faculty.
- Possibility for additional instructional support by using library graduate assistants or English graduate teaching assistants with joint appointments.

Threats

- Teaching faculty burn-out.
- Diminishing library budget (5 percent reduction anticipated over following year).
- Rapidly changing instructional technologies (cost, training, adaptation, assessment).

Environmental scans

The guidelines also advocate that a program plan should "incorporate findings from environmental scans" (ACRL, 2012a). Environmental scans, also taken from the business world, examine external factors. One of the most basic data points for an environmental scan is population/demographic statistics (Lee, 1999). From where do your students come? Are they from urban or rural areas? What are their ages? What is their ethnicity? What is their gender? Are they first-time college students? Colleges and universities regularly collect this information, and it is likely already available through an institutional effectiveness or institutional research office. General demographic data may even be widely accessible via campus web pages. Don't hesitate to ask. Develop a relationship with institutional data officers; they may provide additional data, and for their own reasons are often eager to participate in strategic studies and assessments. In many cases, they might provide personnel expertise and technical assistance to help conduct an environmental scan.

Interpreting large amounts of data can be daunting. Consider drafting an executive summary of the more important facts and figures. Represent these images in tables and graphs; visualization helps to clarify and convey the meaning of numbers quickly (ibid.); see Figures 3.1 and 3.2.

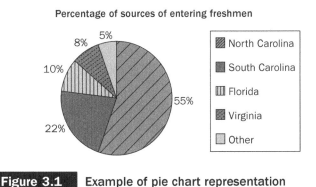

Figure 3.1   Example of pie chart representation

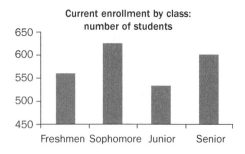

Figure 3.2 Example of bar graph representation

In reviewing the data, look for trends, indicators of change and signs of possible future events within the institution (Morrison, 1992; Koontz, 2006). Use existing professional scans as well. The ACRL Research Planning and Review Committee's most recent environmental scan notably provides readers with a snapshot of national trends (see *http://www. ala.org/acrl/sites/ala.org.acrl/files/content/publications/ whitepapers/EnvironmentalScan201.pdf*). In addition, the ACRL Instruction Section has developed a report, *Analyzing Your Instructional Environment: A Workbook*, to walk you through the process (see *http://www.ala.org/acrl/sites/ala. org.acrl/files/content/aboutacrl/directoryofleadership/ sections/is/iswebsite/projpubs/aie/aie.pdf*).

Needs assessment

Yet another approach to strategic planning is that of conducting a "needs assessment" in order to "identify any existing needs and gaps in ... services and resources" and "provide the library with a focus and a target for continuing or improving its service quality ..." (Mi and Gilbert, 2007: 31). This type of assessment is proactive and can uncover user needs that may be readily apparent. To conduct a needs assessment for an information literacy program one must survey its primary constituents, in this case students and faculty (Altschuld and Witkin, 2000: 9).

Once you have decided to conduct an information literacy needs assessment, what questions should you include? Specific questions are dependent upon institution, but possible examples are shown in Table 3.1.

Table 3.1 Sample needs assessment questions

Factor	Faculty	Students
Demographic	Years at institution? Faculty rank? Highest degree attained.	Class rank? Age? Gender?
Frequency	How often have you scheduled an information literacy session in the past two years? In conjunction with what class?	How often have you attended an information literacy session in the past two years? In conjunction with what class?
Characteristics of session	Did the librarian make use of active and/or collaborative learning? Provide examples. Was the library session based on specific learning outcomes? Did you meet with the librarian to plan the library session?	How did the librarian present information to you? Did the librarian make you aware of the learning goals of the library session?
Information seeking behavior	Do you expect your students to conduct research for your assignments? What sources do you require students to use? What is the number of sources required for assignments.	Where do you go for information for your research assignments? How often do you use library resources? What is the most difficult aspect of using library resources? How often do you ask for help from a librarian?

Include as many open-ended questions as appropriate, based on instruction usage, needs and perception of instruction quality (Mi and Gilbert, 2007: 35). Include an open comments option at the end of each section. Open-ended questions allow users to share important insights and information garnered in this way often provides the most useful feedback. Always end a needs assessment survey with versions of the same two open-ended questions:

What do you like most about the library's instruction program?

or

What are the library's instruction program's strengths?

AND

What do you like least about the library's instruction program? What suggestions do you have for improvement?

or

What are the library's instruction program's weaknesses? What suggestions do you have for improvement?

Pilot the survey, refine it based on initial feedback, and then distribute it to a broader sample (ibid.) Most institutions now have access to versions of online survey instruments, such as SurveyMonkey or Qualtrics. This online survey software is beneficial in that it provides for ease of distribution and participant response, and it allows for the systematic coding of data, which can be reported and collated in a number of different formats. If access to online software is not available, paper surveys, while more labor intensive, are as effective. One word of advice if surveying students: consider an incentive (give-aways, drawings) in order to increase participation (ibid.; Grassian and Kaplowitz, 2009: 114).

Prioritizing assessment results

Once survey data is collected, analyze and prioritize the results. A survey will result in numerous comments and suggestions, from the sacred to the profane. One of my students' needs assessments yielded the need for a coffee and donut bar in the instruction lab. The key lies in identifying what is most important to the greatest number of users, and whose solution is feasible (Altschuld and Witkin, 2000: 113). First, look for frequency of similar responses. If a particular characteristic or aspect of your program consistently receives low scores, this indicates a need for more than one user, as does multiple comments on a specific issue or identified weakness.

The ultimate goal of a needs assessment is to determine what a program can reasonably hope to accomplish (Grassian and Kaplowitz, 2009: 115). There are a number of strategies for ranking results and setting priorities (Mercer and Woolston, 1980; Ashford-Rowe and Holt, 2011). One of the simplest is the "four-square model" (Paparone, 2010). First, create a four-square box and label each square; there are a variety of labels one can use and Figure 3.3 highlights two classic models.

Next, take comments and suggestions and place these within the squares. Ultimately, those comments which fall in the upper-right quadrants are items that should be acted on immediately. Items in the upper-left quadrant should be placed on a "to do" list, and a later time frame developed for their completion. For those items that fall into the lower-right quadrant, attempt to manage them by assigning them to other people, or, at the very least, do not spend much time on their accomplishment. Finally, discard any elements that find their home in the lower-left quadrant. Strategically, you want to focus your efforts on those elements that provide the greatest impact; you do not want to become bogged down in anything which may amount to very little.

Low priority High impact	High priority High impact	Important Not urgent	Urgent Important
Low priority Low impact	High priority Low impact	Not important Not urgent	Urgent Not important

Figure 3.3 Four-square examples

Utilizing focus groups

Assessment literature also suggests using focus or discussion groups to assess needs. Over the course of my career, at different institutions, I have discovered that a good number of administrators absolutely fall in love with this idea. It would appear to be an easy and inexpensive assessment tool. After all, to conduct a focus group, all that is required is a small number of stakeholders sitting around a table and talking – right? In truth, conducting effective and valid focus groups requires significant time and expertise. For several months prior to entering graduate school, I worked as an assistant in a marketing research firm whose primary clientele were politicians and consumer product companies. I participated in a variety of projects that used online telephone surveys and face-to-face product testing, and I worked closely with the lead facilitator on three focus groups. I observed first-hand the time and effort required to develop these focus group projects from start to finish.

One of the primary pitfalls when convening focus or discussion groups is objectivity. Ten years ago, the dean of my library decided it was time to hold three focus groups, one each for faculty, undergraduates and graduate students. While a group on campus was able to facilitate for a fee, the administrator decided on a "do-it-yourself" approach. Needless to say, the results were unusable. The staff member tasked with facilitating the groups, however well-intentioned, was ill-equipped to lead the project. I took notes during all three sessions. Well-designed questions were not prepared: "So, what's wrong with the library?" was the lead question. During the third session, all discussion came to a stop. After goading the group to talk, my co-worker decided to fill the silence with what *she thought* was amiss in the library. Should the decision be made to pursue focus and discussion groups, I cannot recommend strongly enough that you insist on an outside provider with professional expertise in the craft (Morgan, 1998a, 1998b; Harley et al., 2006).

Conclusion

Now you have crafted a mission statement, developed general program goals and objectives, collected data from various sources, conducted a needs assessment, and prioritized stakeholder needs. The journey has begun, but it is not yet complete. The following chapters will aid in expanding and adding other components of a program plan: administrative and institutional support, articulation within the curriculum, collaboration, pedagogy, staffing, outreach and assessment.

4

Packing for the journey: administrative and institutional support

Abstract: Appropriate levels of administrative and institutional support, including well-defined roles and responsibilities, as well as funding and budgetary support, are critical to the success of an information literacy program.

Key words: program leadership, program responsibilities, institutional support, administrative support, funding, budget.

Administrative support

Librarians' enthusiasm, dedication and commitment can carry an information literacy program to a certain extent. Without the proper support from supervisors and administrators, however, improvement and growth will be constrained. Let us be frank, managers and superiors are also capable of a lack of understanding, unrealistic expectations and bouts of magical thinking. Librarians do battle with a number of bureaucratic attitudes towards information literacy programs. There are administrators who believe that information technology advances either substitute for education or render traditional education models and even physical campuses useless. Some administrators hold the view that everyone has equal access to technology – another technology trap. In contrast to those enamored with technology are those who refuse to embrace even the best of technology (Bundy, 1999). Many supervisors have had no teaching experience, or are so far away from being in the classroom that they do not understand how long it takes to plan and prepare for a teaching session. A historian friend of mine likes to complain that "administration is the enemy." To build a successful information literacy program that reaches its full potential, do what you can to make your administrators your friends.

Designated roles and responsibilities

Librarians, therefore, must effectively and routinely communicate and advocate program needs to their bosses in ways that encourage them to support an information literacy program. The place to start, if possible, is by reminding them of what they need to do when hiring and staffing. According to the *Characteristics*, administrators should provide support in several ways. Initially, they do so by:

- Assigning information literacy leadership and responsibilities to appropriate librarians, faculty and staff.

(ACRL, 2012a)

By simply designating a person to lead an information literacy program, administrators first convey the program's importance within the organization and to external stakeholders. Any subsequent hires reinforce the importance of the program. They say, "information literacy is here to stay." The assignment should detail responsibilities and reporting lines clearly, charging authority for oversight, continuity and quality. Further specifications should be described within a job description. If program responsibilities are only part of the overall role, then percentages of time and commitment must also be articulated in order to avoid confusion and friction. With any responsibility comes accountability, thus job performance must be evaluated at some level. If an evaluation program is in place already, it should be modified to recognize information literacy duties.

Hiring – qualities

Here, a word to administrators might be appropriate. Who should you be hiring or tasking to lead information literacy programs? What characteristics should candidates possess? In addition to the appropriate library education and experience, Grassian and Kaplowitz – in their inspirational and encouraging book, *Learning to Lead and Manage Information Literacy Instruction* (2005) – identify four foundational qualities for leaders: vision, passion, courage and integrity.

Vision is knowing where a program needs to go and having the ability to share that plan, providing motivation and direction so that "everyone knows where to go and why" (Grassian and Kaplowitz, 2005: 9).

Passion is also required; one must truly care and believe in the program's mission and in the value of its outcomes (ibid.: 11). Passion inspires others and its importance cannot be denied. Earlier in my career, I reported to an instruction coordinator whose "passion" was limited to keeping exact and detailed statistics; scant attention was paid to any other aspect of the instruction program. When all that mattered were the number of classes delivered and the number of students taught, it was difficult for my colleagues and me to value much else.

Courage is another essential component of leadership. It is the conviction of vision, coupled with passion, which results in action, and sometimes in forging a new path without permission. While relationships should not be adversarial, there are instances when program leaders must fight for what is right. Sometimes the word "no" simply is the appropriate response. Of course, this courage, or fearlessness, must be tempered with a "healthy dose of patience" (ibid.: 12), and a good leader finds ways to "win" without blatant confrontation.

Integrity is the final leadership quality. Good leaders manage by example, and their actions are consistent and based on unwavering personal values. It might be difficult to list the above four qualities as requirements in a traditional position announcement, but administrators should look for evidence of these qualities within an applicant's pack, and seek out anecdotal confirmation during the job interview. Grassian and Kaplowitz also list an additional set of characteristics which define leaders, and these include the abilities to communicate persuasively, encourage diversity, take risks, build relationships and seek learning opportunities (ibid.: 14–15).

Hiring – proficiencies

In addition, the ACRL *Standards for Proficiencies for Instruction Librarians and Coordinators* (see Appendix 4) also list a number of characteristics, or proficiencies, required for *all* librarians who participate in information literacy instruction at any level. The desired skill sets include many "skills" indeed: administrative skills, assessment and evaluation skills, communication skills, curriculum knowledge, information literacy integration skills, instructional design skills, leadership skills, planning skills, presentation skills, promotion skills, subject expertise and teaching skills. For program leaders, or coordinators, these proficiencies include the same skills, signifying higher levels of mastery, leadership and oversight (see also Appendix 4).

Support in word and deed

Documentation

- Incorporating information literacy in the institution's missions, strategic plan, policies and procedures.

(ACRL, 2012a)

This best practice for administrators speaks for itself. Program leaders must make use of any and every opportunity to promote and urge leadership to think about and cite information literacy within library and campus documents. Without such continued advocacy, it may be easy for administrators to overlook the program.

Funding

- Providing funding to establish and ensure ongoing support for teaching facilities, current and appropriate technologies, appropriate staffing levels and professional development.

(ACRL, 2012a)

In these days of shrinking and strained library budgets, adequate monetary support for most programs is difficult to obtain and maintain. Keeping information literacy program funding at the fore requires a continual effort. It is difficult for many of us to ask for money, but, in this case, being the proverbial "squeaky wheel" is a good strategy. Several other strategies come to mind with regard to budgeting.

For example, when requesting funding, remember always to justify a request by illustrating the value of information literacy for students and faculty. Suggest that the funding of an instruction position or classroom technology could be used as a marketing tool, demonstrating to external constituents the library's commitment to, and partnership with, student education. Be prepared to describe how the program adds value to the library's overall mission and goals, and ultimately to the institution as a whole.

Look for opportunities to maximize budget requests as well. For instance, if a library is undergoing renovation it may be a good time to ask for upgrades to a computer lab or teaching space. When physical changes need to be made, most administrators would prefer to bundle costs at the same time. Ask for permission to sit in on budget discussions. If you are unable to participate, be aware of when those discussions are taking place and ask your supervisor to make the case for you. Be sure to supply the justification and supporting evidence too. If possible, become an advocate for a separate information literacy instruction budget. A separate budget allows a measure of program control, and administrators may be content not to have to deal with every office supply request that may come their way.

Be creative when making requests. If an initial request is denied, be prepared to follow it up with a lower-cost substitution. It is good strategy to go to an administrator and acknowledge that while he or she was unable to fund a project at a particular level, there are ways to accomplish the particular goal with a reasonable and less costly alternative.

Maintain an up-to-date "wish list" of items needed, from inexpensive supply items or promotional materials to classroom support technology, or to conference registration, or to big-ticket requests such as computer labs or additional instruction positions. Befriend library or institutional development officers. Talk with them about the importance of an information literacy program and make sure they have an updated desiderata list for your program. Never be caught short if a funding opportunity suddenly becomes available.

External funding

Finally, look for external funding and grant opportunities. Most colleges and universities offer in-house grants geared towards teacher effectiveness and training. At my home university, our Center for Teaching Excellence awards money to applicants who propose projects that directly benefit teachers or students. Through this avenue, we were able to secure funding for the production of online help videos (Auburn University Libraries, 2012) and the publication of a web evaluation training booklet for composition instructors. Be aware of unconventional opportunities as well. As part of an English composition revision, the composition coordinator asked our librarians to help select the majority of articles for a locally produced class reader. The coordinator, pleased with our participation, decided to reward our time and expertise by setting aside a portion of the reader profits to subvent the costs of information literacy workshops for composition instructors. The instruction program was unable to collect the money directly, but the funds were used to pay for workshop space in the student union and provide lunches or refreshments for the sessions.

Asking for money can be an uncomfortable exercise and requires some of the courage we discussed earlier in the chapter. It does become easier over time. The sooner one begins to solicit funding, the sooner a successful request.

Collaborative and campus-wide support

- Recognizing and encouraging collaboration (see also Chapter 5).

(ACRL, 2012a)

Library administrators interact with other administrators across a campus and can serve as an important ally in integrating information literacy at an institutional level. Support at this higher level is crucial. Administrators can initiate conversations and talk about information literacy with other program coordinators, deans, vice-presidents, provosts and presidents. Administrators pave the way for you across campus.

- Communicating support for the program.
- Rewarding individual and institutional achievement and participation in the information literacy program.

(ACRL, 2012a)

Conclusion

Ultimately, administrators can communicate support by incorporating information literacy into the library's overall mission, by providing adequate funding and by voicing advocacy at an institutional level. In terms of rewards, most of us would like a nice raise, of course. Sadly, in this difficult economic climate with lay-offs, mandated furloughs and forced leave without pay, salary increases may be completely unattainable. In the short term, however, there are alternative kinds of monetary rewards other than a direct pay increase, such as administrative funding to attend workshops or conferences and paid release-time for professional development and/or research.

Administrative and institutional support takes many different forms. It may be incumbent upon those involved with an information literacy program to help those in administrative roles understand the nature and requirements of information literacy and the need for a strong program. Librarians must advocate for information literacy as a principle, highlighting its value to students and the academy, and being definite about personnel and budgetary needs. Administrative and institutional support is vital, as is the support of our main constituents, students and faculty.

5

Articulation and collaboration

Abstract: An information literacy program does not operate in a vacuum, and its success is dependent on how well the program meets educational and academic needs. In addition, the support of key partners, most notably faculty, is critical. By situating instruction offerings within the curriculum and by working collaboratively with classroom faculty, the instruction program will become a vital and essential part of students' overall education experience.

Key words: program articulation, collaboration, partnerships.

An essential pairing

When the American Civil War began, soldiers' tents were large and heavy. The so-called Sibley tent, for example, was a canvas version of the Western teepee, capable of housing between 12 and 20 men. Such shelters were weighty, cumbersome and took up a great deal of space in army wagons. If the wagon train was delayed by rain or mud, soldiers ended up sleeping in the open air. Eventually, the Union Army developed more portable protection called the shelter-half. Each man received a rectangle of canvas, 5'2" × 4'8". At night, two soldiers buttoned their shelter-halves together to make a tent. They would throw it over a

SHADED SHELTERS.

Figure 5.1 "Shaded shelters"

Source: Billings, 1887

ridge pole or sometimes simply a rope tied between two trees. The structure that resulted was so small that many soldiers complained that it was hardly big enough for a dog, hence the name "dog tent" or, eventually, "pup tent," or, elsewhere, shelter-half (see Figure 5.1). But by cooperating and planning nightly, soldiers on the march developed ways to stay dry.

Articulation

First-year experience

The *Characteristics* list articulation and collaboration as two separate categories, but, much like the two pieces of the original pup tent, the two are interdependent. An information literacy program can succeed only if both halves are present. In beginning to build articulation, librarians should first look to their institution's basic curricular sequence: first-/freshman-year experience (FYE), core/general education and major course work. FYE offerings are commonly described as classes or programs whose goals are to help incoming students make the transition from high school to college life, both academically and socially (Barefoot, 2005; Brinkworth et al., 2009). Students themselves recognize that they are unprepared and acknowledge that some of their high-school classes were not educationally challenging, thus impeding the development of good study and test-taking habits. In terms of information literacy, students appreciate that while they could find information in high school, the information-seeking strategies and materials selected for high-school papers and reports might not meet academic "standards of accuracy and academic rigor" (Barefoot, 2005). Students who for the first time are responsible for their own schedules also hopefully understand the need for better time-management skills (Rausch and Hamilton, 2006: 326–7).

The FYE curriculum helps "shape [the] academic identity of incoming students" (Bissett, 2004: 12). Another goal of FYE is to provide students with a friendly, ready-made cohort, resulting in students feeling less isolated (Peel, 2000; Rausch and Hamilton, 2006: 327). Students who participate in FYE develop and hone the foundation skills necessary to meet the more rigorous demands of higher education and to develop a social network, both factors which contribute to successful matriculation. Colleges and universities certainly benefit from early student success – retention rates are higher for those students who reach their second year, as is the overall graduation rate (Horn and Carroll, 1998). Retention and graduation rates are of critical concern for institutions of higher learning. Some 79 percent of first-time, full-time students and 45 percent of first-time, part-time students who entered four-year program institutions in 2009 returned the following year to continue their studies (this percentage indicates the retention rate). At two-year program institutions, the retention rate for those who first entered school in 2009 was 61 percent for full-time students and 42 percent for part-time students (National Center for Education Statistics (NCES), 2011). Institutions have a vested interest in improving those statistics.

Topics typically covered in the FYE curriculum include: study habits, note taking, test-taking strategies, health awareness (nutrition, sex, drug and alcohol information), community and public service, personal ethics, academic integrity and plagiarism ... and information literacy (Boff and Johnson, 2002; Karshmer and Bryan, 2011). Another typical FYE course might focus on an introduction to the institution itself, and components might include learning the history of the school, navigating campus buildings, participating in campus events, and even learning the school alma mater and fight songs.

The actual structures of FYE offerings vary greatly from school to school. The number of credits awarded range from one to three. Some are mandatory while others are optional; to earn credits students might receive a pass/fail or a letter grade. The good news, according to a recent study, is that a large majority of FYEs include some kind of information component and an equally large majority of librarians are involved in teaching (Boff and Johnson, 2002; Hardesty, 2007; Johnson et al., 2008).

The core curriculum

Some institutions also situate freshmen writing or composition classes within an FYE program of study. The majority of colleges and universities, however, include English composition, usually as a two-semester sequence, within a core or general education curriculum (Varner et al., 1996; Jacobson and Mackey, 2007; Zoellner et al., 2008; Maitaouthong et al., 2010/2011). It is within the English writing core that librarians have been most successful in incorporating basic information literacy skills, as students are asked to complete a research paper (Jacobs and Jacobs, 2009). Core literature class assignments also require students to carry out research, and allow librarians to reiterate basic information literacy skills as well as to introduce students to subject-based resources. "Public Speaking" or "Introduction to Communication" assignments usually require students to support their speeches and presentations with credible and reliable documentation – another opportunity to reinforce basic information literacy skills. Many colleges still maintain the requirement for a core computer technology course, and while the focus tends towards the technical aspects of using computers, many include a component on the Internet and may also touch on website evaluation. Science, technology, engineering and math (STEM) core classes commonly focus on practical skills and applications and it is difficult for librarians to find an entry into these courses at the general education level, although it may be possible to integrate information literacy within specific research projects (Liu and Sun, 2011). Once students complete their core requirements and begin their coursework for their majors, research-intensive assignments require more sophisticated information literacy skills and a familiarity with academic, scholarly and subject-specific resources. For many majors, students must also successfully complete a capstone course with an assignment (written paper or research project) that demonstrates the accomplishment of a set of curriculum content and learning objectives. History majors at my institution, for example, must research and write an article-length paper based on primary sources. Evidence-based practical curriculums, such as nursing, may also offer an opportunity to integrate information literacy at the core level (Blankenship and Fox, 1998).

A basic, overall sequence for the curriculum thus progresses from FYE offerings, to core or general education classes, to major classes. This progression is logical, and for many librarians the introduction of information literacy skills and competencies at each stage appears just as straightforward. It is simple and uncomplicated if one assumes that information literacy is a one-shot, one-size-fits-all instruction session, or that all that is needed are slight adjustments to a standard, "canned" library orientation.

Articulation defined

The *Characteristics*, however, are clear; articulation within the curriculum for an information literacy program:

- identifies the scope (i.e., depth and complexity) of competencies to be acquired on a disciplinary level as well as a course level; and

- sequences and integrates competencies throughout a student's academic career, progressing in sophistication.

(ACRL, 2012a)

In other words, a cookie-cutter approach to information literacy does not work. Too often I have seen librarians fail to correctly interpret depth, complexity and sophistication. For example, to meet this goal, librarians structure a FYE library session to include an orientation to the library's homepage, the library online catalog and general databases.

To raise the level for a senior history course the librarian would only vary the session slightly, with another orientation to the library's homepage, another introduction to the library online catalog and a review of subject-specific history databases. Similarly, librarians sometimes assume that offering a library session covering the same subject-specific databases for all classes within a discipline is appropriate. At a former institution, one librarian offered the same library instruction class to every literature class, regardless of class level or assignment. After four years, students were able to mimic the librarian's session almost word-for-word, including examples used and jokes told. Not surprisingly, they complained with each successive class about "going to the library … ."

What the *Characteristics* actually require is much more difficult to accomplish, and necessitates an understanding of learner-centered learning and student learning outcomes (see issues of pedagogy in Chapter 7) as well as an understanding of a holistic, information literacy plan outside of a single class or subject.

Curriculum mapping

So what might this articulation look like? There are several different forms, but, in general, each details a specific learning outcome or competency, and then maps the outcome to a particular class or course. In addition, the articulation might also note the level of student development, and include activities and assessments. This process may also be defined as "curriculum mapping" (Glass, 2007; Hale, 2008) and two examples can be found in Tables 5.1 and 5.2.

Table 5.1 Curriculum mapping – Example 1

Outcome	Class	Level
Identifies key concepts and terms that describe the information need; identifies key words, synonyms and related terms for the information needed.	ENGL 1120 (first session)	Introductory

Table 5.2 Curriculum mapping – Example 2

Outcome	Class	Level	Activity	Assessment
Investigates the scope, content and organization of information retrieval systems.	HIST 3600	Intermediate	Teams will be formed to investigate the scope of five different history databases, complete a worksheet answering specific scope-related questions and present findings to class.	Worksheets will be collected and graded against rubric.

In this way, and as according to the *Characteristics*, the plan specifies programs and courses charged with implementing competencies and specific information literacy learning outcomes. Once the plan has been articulated, the Guidelines suggest that the plan be formalized and disseminated widely, and used by stakeholders for advocacy and to integrate information literacy campus-wide. If possible, a representative of the program will participate in the faculty governance that oversees programs and curriculum. While the library itself is not a program, a viable argument can be made to administrators that the library serves as a critical academic unit, and that its expertise and support is vital to student success.

Collaboration

The *Oxford English Dictionary* defines "collaborate" as:

> To work in conjunction with another or others, to co-operate; esp. in a literary or artistic production, or the like.

> (*OED* Online, 2012)

While one can articulate and plan, without collaboration an articulation plan is simply words on paper, and cannot be put into action. At times, it is difficult to determine which came first, much like the proverbial chicken-and-egg debate. Which comes first – articulation or collaboration? It varies. Collaboration may have first initiated an articulation. Or, librarians may have developed a plan and taken it to faculty. Our collaborations with faculty are critical. In reality, "teaching faculty are not only the primary deliverers of instruction, but are also usually in control of decisions about curricula" (Van Cleave, 2007: 181). There is little doubt that the success of an information literacy program is dependent upon collaboration with faculty. While librarians often take a leadership role within information literacy, without the cooperation of regular teaching faculty librarians are unable to move information literacy forward.

Classroom faculty collaboration

How do faculty view information literacy? In a recent study, survey results indicate that faculty are indeed concerned about their students' information literacy skills, particularly among lower-level undergraduates. The same study also suggests that faculty believe information is important. In addition, while a majority of faculty thought that information literacy instruction should be undertaken collaboratively, just over half of the respondents actually participated in information literacy instruction (Bury, 2011). In another recent study, similar results were noted: faculty rated information literacy as important, agreed that teaching information literacy was a shared responsibility, and were concerned about their students' information literacy skills (Saunders, 2012).

Knowing this about faculty suggests that approaching faculty, and engaging in a conversation about their students' work, is a good place to start a dialog about collaborating on information literacy instruction (Van Cleave, 2007: 181). Remind faculty that studies suggest that participation in information literacy sessions tends to result in better papers, in students putting more effort into locating sources, and in bibliographies that contain better and more relevant sources (Millet et al., 2009: 163). In addition, working with faculty at an individual level may also allow for collaboration on assignments (Ellison, 2004), and for shaping those assignments to be fully integrated into an information literacy curriculum (Mazella et al., 2011).

Collaborations and partnerships are formed in a variety of ways: formally and informally, personally and professionally. No matter how the collaboration is formed, however, "all successful and sustained partnerships are characterized by common strategic elements: shared mission, complimentary skills for mutual benefit, strong communication and organizational structures" (Noe and MacEwan, 2010: 106). In addition to individual faculty members, librarians must also target key personnel such as program coordinators and directors, as well as department heads and chairs. Look for those who have some direct and overall curricular responsibility.

Campus partners

Opportunities for collaboration also exist outside of the formal class and curricula framework. There are a number of natural partners, bolstered in part by the "Commons" initiatives. Writing centers and other tutoring services, such as peer-to-peer student academic tutoring, lead to information literacy specialists serving as tutors and providing information literacy training and development to other professional and student tutoring staff. Consider working with student communities such as Residence Life, partnering with study or tutoring groups situated in residence halls or dormitories (Ruediger and Neal, 2004). By their very nature, learning and/or living communities are shaped around a shared learning or cohabitation experience, and provide librarians with opportunities for interaction (Van Cleave, 2007). Librarians benefit by getting to know those leading the communities, as well as the students themselves, on a personal level, which may help to change attitudes towards librarians and allow students themselves to become information literacy advocates (Ruediger and Neal, 2004).

Look for campus-wide projects or initiatives as well. As discussed above, freshmen writing and English composition classes seem like natural places for information literacy instruction. Programs such as Writing across the Curriculum (WAC) (Elmborg, 2003; D'Angelo and Maid, 2004; Johnson et al., 2008) or Writing in the Disciplines (WID) (Ovadia,

2010) also serve as natural extensions for the writing/research/ information literacy paradigm. Some institutions are now creating undergraduate research and awards programs, which may open the door for information literacy dialog (Bodemer, 2012). For institutions under the auspices of the Southern Association of Colleges and Schools (SACS), for example, the accreditation process requires the inclusion of a Quality Enhancement Plan (QEP). In addition to broad writing programs, other QEP initiatives may include critical thinking, FYE programming and even information literacy itself (Millet et al., 2009) (see also the SACS website: *http://www.sacscoc. org/2010TrackbQEPSummaries.asp*). Of course, the best time to begin integrating information literacy into any campus-wide program is at the outset. These initiatives take two–three years from development to practice (Miller, 2010) – so if you are unable to contribute at the very beginning, join the process as soon as possible, or when feasible.

Does your institution have a Center for Teaching Excellence for Teacher Training and Development (Iannuzzi, 1998)? Often, such initiatives are interested in partnering with any number of campus experts, and willingly advertise and host workshops, seminars and brown-bag luncheons on a variety of topics. From my own experience, those who work in development centers are most eager to have librarians speak to fellow faculty on information literacy. Consider the benefits of information literacy as faculty development (Frier et al., 2001); faculty receive valuable information, and make a personal connection for future collaboration. Not all collaboration is curriculum and classroom driven, however, and technology too can play a role in collaboration. Librarians should make available resource pages, tutorials, videos or information literacy learning modules for use within course management systems (CMSs) and learning management systems (LMSs) (Van Cleave, 2007: 183).

Conclusion

Successful articulation and collaboration efforts go a long way towards meeting the *Characteristics'* components of fostering communication among disciplinary faculty, librarians and other instructors such as graduate assistants, as well as administrators and other staff within the institution. They enhance student learning and skill development for lifelong learning, communicating effectively to gain support for the program within the academic community, aligning information literacy within disciplinary content, and working within the context of the course content and other learning experiences to achieve information literacy outcomes and to place at different stages, planning, delivery, assessment of student learning and evaluation and refinement of the program.

6

Today's (and tomorrow's) student

Abstract: While all students bring their own individual experiences, perceptions and skills into the classroom, it is important for educators to attempt to learn more about our students. Collecting demographic information, reviewing research on generational characteristics and learning as much as possible about the ways in which they think, learn and interact with the world can only help to strengthen our efforts as we meet them in the classroom.

Key words: student demographics, student characteristics, Generation X, Generation Y, Generation Next, iGeneration.

Knowing our students

Knowing our numbers (demographics)

As crucial as administrators and faculty are to the success of an information literacy program, the other critical constituents – students – warrant a great deal of consideration. If I could add to the *Characteristics*, I would include a component that suggests a more holistic understanding of students, one based on social and cultural information. What do we know about today's undergraduate students? Let's start with some basics. The National Center for

Education Statistics (NCES), a beneficial source for up-to-date statistical data and projections, notes the following:

- Between 2000 and 2010, undergraduate enrollment in degree-granting postsecondary institutions increased by 37 percent, from 13.2 to 18.1 million students. Projections indicate that undergraduate enrollment will continue to increase, reaching 20.6 million students in 2021.

- During 2000 to 2010, male enrollment grew 36 percent, from 5.8 million to 7.8 million students, while female enrollment grew 39 percent, from 7.4 to 10.2 million students. In 2010, females accounted for 57 percent of undergraduate enrollment, and males, 43 percent. Enrollments for both males and females are expected to increase through 2021, reaching 8.6 and 12.0 million students, respectively.

- Of the 18 million undergraduate students at degree-granting institutions in the United States in fall 2010, some 76 percent attended public institutions, 15 percent attended private nonprofit colleges and universities, and 10 percent attended private for-profit institutions.

- Undergraduate enrollment in public institutions increased from 10.5 million students in 2000 to 13.7 million in 2010, a 30 percent increase. Private institutions experienced a higher rate of growth over this period, increasing 67 percent, from 2.6 to 4.4 million students. Most of the growth in private institution enrollment between 2000 and 2010 occurred at for-profit institutions – their enrollment increased more than 300 percent, from 0.4 to

1.7 million students. Enrollment at private nonprofit institutions increased by 20 percent, from 2.2 to 2.7 million students.

- Between 2000 and 2010, undergraduate enrollment at 4-year institutions increased from 7.2 to 10.4 million students and is expected to reach 11.8 million in 2021.

- Enrollment increased 34 percent (from 4.8 to 6.5 million) at public 4-year institutions, 22 percent at private nonprofit 4-year institutions (from 2.2 to 2.6 million), and 513 percent at private for-profit 4-year institutions (from 0.2 to 1.3 million).

- During the same period, enrollment at 2-year institutions increased from 5.9 to 7.7 million students and is expected to reach 8.8 million students by 2021. Between 2000 and 2010, enrollment decreased 44 percent at private nonprofit 2-year institutions (from 59,000 to 33,000) and increased 124 percent at private for-profit 2-year institutions (from 192,000 to 430,000) and 26 percent at public 2-year institutions (from 5.7 to 7.2 million).

- Undergraduate enrollment of U.S. residents generally increased between 1980 and 2010 for each racial/ethnic group. By 2010, the number of White students had grown to 10.9 million (62 percent.) The number of Black undergraduate students who were U.S. residents increased 163 percent between 1980 and 2010, from 1.0 million (10 percent) to 2.7 million students (15 percent). Hispanic and Asian/Pacific Islander enrollments increased 487 and 337 percent, respectively, from 1980 to 2010 (14 and 6 percent in 2010). American Indian/Alaska Native enrollment increased from 78,000 to 179,000 students from 1980 to 2010 (1 percent of total enrollment in each year). There were about 294,000 undergraduate students who were of two or more races in 2010. In previous years, these students were included in the other racial/ethnic groups.

- In 2010, about 40 percent of full-time and 73 percent of part-time college students aged 16 to 24 were employed; a higher percentage of female full-time students were employed than were male full-time students (42 vs. 37 percent). A higher percentage of White students were employed (44 percent) than were Hispanic, Black or Asian students (35 percent, 33 percent and 30 percent, respectively).

(National Center for Education Statistics, 2011)

The trend is worldwide. According to the 2012 report on education from the Organisation for Economic Co-operation and Development (OECD), which surveys higher education and adults learners internationally:

- Efforts to raise people's level of education have led to significant changes in attainment, particularly at the top and bottom ends of the education spectrum. In 1997, on average across OECD countries, 36% of 25–64-year-olds had not completed upper secondary education, 43% had completed upper secondary or post-secondary non-tertiary education, and another 21% had completed tertiary education. By 2010, the proportion of adults who had not attained an upper secondary education had fallen by 10 percentage points; the proportion with a tertiary degree had risen by 10 percentage points.

- Across almost all OECD countries, upper secondary attainment is the norm. On average, 74% of 25–64-year-olds have reached this level of attainment, and 82% of 25–34-year-olds have.

- Tertiary attainment levels have increased considerably over the past 30 years. On average across OECD countries, 38% of 25–34-year-olds have a tertiary attainment.

- Vocational attainment tends to be strongest in countries that have historically emphasized this kind of education or have well-established apprenticeship systems. However, vocational education is a significant part of the education systems in many other countries as well. In an additional 10 OECD countries, a vocational upper secondary or post-secondary non-tertiary attainment is the highest educational level for more than 30% of 25–64-year-olds.

(Source: *http://www.oecd.org/edu/EAG%202012_e-book_EN_200912.pdf*)

What does it all mean? Overall, student populations are growing rapidly, especially at the much-ballyhooed for-profit schools, but also at more traditional institutions. Student populations are unique at every institution, of course, and demographic data for a single college or university may or may not reflect national statistics and trends. But, in general, students are infinitely more diverse – culturally, ethnically, educationally and socio-economically – than ever before.

In addition to reviewing basic demographic information for student populations nationally, one should look at what an individual institution has to offer. Yours probably collects data on topics as varied as declared majors, first-generation college students, non-native English speakers, and whether or not students are working full time or part time (Kangas et al., 2000). All of this can help get a sense of the students in your classrooms. Note that these data points change at a rapid rate, and so it is important to gather and interpret data annually. Otherwise it is quite easy for one year's statistical data to become part of a persistent and pervasive institutional narrative, which once in place may be difficult to dislodge. Ten years ago, for example, at my home institution, demographics indicated that a vast majority of our students were coming from within the state. However, our enrollment a decade later shows that the overall number of these students has decreased significantly, and trends indicate that within a few years in-state applicants may only comprise half of those enrolled. Demographics like these alone do not tell the entire story of a student population, but they do provide a fairly accurate snapshot and a starting point in understanding who students are.

Knowing our student characteristics

In addition to compiling and interpreting statistical data, other sources of information are available. Educators over the last few decades have endeavored to characterize students generationally, detailing common habits, traits and personalities by age and/or decade. Terms such as "Baby Boomers," "Gen X," and "Generation Y" (aka "Milliennials") all mark attempts to label and describe a certain demographic cohort. Pop culture clichés aside, in many ways these broad definitions, and many of the characteristics associated with them, may seem to fit. Unfortunately, research conducted on Milliennials, i.e., those students born between 1980 and 2000 (Rainer and Rainer, 2011), tends to focus on the more negative connotations of the generation. Even the titles of recent, well-received and heavily referenced works such as *Generation Me* (Twenge, 2006) and *The Dumbest Generation* (Bauerlein, 2008) clearly project the overall theme and sentiment of the work. I think more useful are those works that, while still outlining some of the challenges of working with Millennials, tend to focus on more positive aspects and attempt to offer suggestions of how best to work with students of this particular generation (Montana and Petit, 2008; Bonner et al., 2011; Rainer and Rainer, 2011). There is now an attempt to label the next generation, i.e., those students born after the turn of the twenty-first century. Scholars have yet to settle on the perfect label, and continue to look for research dealing with Generation Z (Dillon, 2007; Tulgan, 2012), iGeneration or Generation iY (Elmore, 2010).

Should your institute participate, data from a National Survey of Student Engagement (NSSE) study may also help to complete the picture of your students. This instrument asks students to respond to questions that cover:

- *Academic challenge*: including higher-order learning, reflective and integrative learning, quantitative reasoning and learning strategies.
- *Learning with peers*: including collaborative learning and discussions with diverse others.
- *Experiences with faculty*: including student–faculty interaction and teaching practices.
- *Campus environment*: including quality of interactions and supportive environment.
- *High-impact practices*: special undergraduate opportunities such as service-learning, study abroad, research with faculty and internships that have substantial positive effects on student learning and retention.

(Source: *http://nsse.iub.edu/*)

Most crucially, research tends to confirm what many of us involved in information literacy already know at an anecdotal level: the majority of students who come to us are under-prepared. There are many reasons as to why this is so. There are a number of additional challenges for community college students that include a lack of both research and technology skills (Martin and Petitfils, 2010). These students represent a constituency of "diverse learners who have competing priorities" (Warren, 2006: 300). They balance school work with personal life issues and financial and family responsibilities, such as employment, childcare and elderly family care. Even when community college students decide to transfer to a four-year institution, they still find themselves under-prepared, particularly in math and writing (Tipton and Bender, 2006). These challenges are not exclusive to community college students, however. Sadly, the lack of, and low-level mastery of, information literacy and research skills among undergraduate students is prevalent, and cuts across all class levels and disciplines (Pinto, 2012).

Students and technology

And then there is the Internet. We all know that students rely heavily on the Internet for both personal and educational information (Porter, 2011), and they do little to evaluate the reliability and credibility of their sources. Nor do they verify information found (Metzger et al., 2003; Jones et al., 2008). Perhaps one of the reasons students elect not to verify information is that they are simply looking for bits of information, or sentences, which confirm their beliefs or thesis, or which provide a quotation in support of a predetermined argument (Howard et al., 2010). The Citation Project (*http://site.citationproject.net/*), a research project to gather empirical data on how students synthesize sources in an effort to address plagiarism, finds this to be typical student practice. An over-reliance on the Internet, compounded by the ease of copying and pasting (Jones et al., 2008), also contributes to the growing issue of plagiarism. This correlates directly with the ACRL Information Literacy Standard Five: "The information literate student understands many of the economic, legal, and social issues surrounding the use of information and accesses and uses information ethically and legally" (ACRL, 2000: 14).

Further, studies indicate that students are unable to formulate sophisticated search strategies and rarely employ appropriate Boolean operators. Once students identify key words, there is a tendency to continue using those same key words or phrases, even if they produce few or inappropriate results. Rather than revise a key word search strategy using different synonyms, or combinations of key words, students simply go to another tool and attempt the same search (Holman, 2011).

Students have a tendency to overestimate their information literacy and research skill levels. Some studies indicate an overconfidence in student skill sets as students seem to gauge success simply by finding any information, without understanding that there are skills involved in the process of locating the most useful sources (Gross and Latham, 2009). Other studies suggest a more moderate self-perception (Pinto, 2012). Students may conflate technology or computer literacy with information literacy. While they certainly are able to "surf the Net," one recent study suggests that students lack even basic computer competencies (Wallace and Clariana, 2005). Interestingly, incoming standardized test scores do not translate into information literate students (Gross and Latham, 2009: 337), a phenomenon anecdotally reported by my own colleagues and faculty.

Conclusion

While some may see the overall picture as discouraging, I prefer to view the state of student information literacy as any number of opportunities to help students learn and develop the skills they need. To do otherwise is to do a disservice to our students. In reality, individual students do not necessarily fit neatly and nicely within particular groups, or even fit within our own assumptions. We must move beyond those assumptions. In the next chapter, we will discuss how to assess your students' information literacy abilities in order to provide them with the best possible information literacy instruction program.

7

Pedagogy, or "I'm a librarian, not a teacher!"

Abstract: Librarians often do not perceive themselves as natural teachers, yet information literacy requires best practice in teaching. Drawing from the field of education, librarians (and their students) will benefit from an examination of their personal teaching style, the development and implementation of improved pedagogies and class planning, and an awareness of how students learn best.

Key words: pedagogy, teaching styles, learning styles, lesson plans.

What is pedagogy?

Two years ago I taught an English composition class. I selected representative materials from four different types of resources, placed them in baskets, divided the class into groups and gave each group a basket. I asked the group to describe the content, explain the purpose of the items found, identify the likely audience and determine why the types of resources were, or were not, relevant to their class assignment. I then tasked each group to share their findings with the entire class. As I walked around the classroom and checked in with each group, I also observed their discussions. In planning for the class, I had decided on a particular order for the presentations, but based on what I saw I quickly rethought the order. When I informed one group that they would be going first, a student in another group objected. "Our group wants to go first," he declared, "we're done and ready to go!" I replied that my decision wasn't personal, it was pedagogical. "Peda-what?" he asked. I spelled "pedagogy" and suggested he look it up as the other groups were finishing. In an instant he was looking at online dictionaries and eventually settled on a Wikipedia entry. The student watched me intently throughout the remainder of the session. After class, he was the last to leave, and he stopped me at the door to ask if all teachers knew about this thing called "pedagogy." I replied that I thought the good ones did. He looked at me, nodded a couple of times as only the young can, and said, "Cool."

Pedagogy is defined as "the art, occupation, or practice of teaching. Also: the theory or principles of education; a method of teaching based on such a theory" (*OED* Online, 2012). Those teaching at the college and university level have earned advanced degrees in specific subject areas. Coursework at the masters- and doctoral-level curricula focuses on content, and the breadth and depth of knowledge and research required to become expert in a particular field. What few graduate students experience, however, is a systematic study of pedagogy, and so they may have only a passing awareness of the art of teaching. Other than personal experience gained in overfull classrooms, few have the opportunity to formally learn educational and cognitive theory, and may simply not know about the most effective ways to help students learn.

Librarians and pedagogy

The same is not true of librarians. Based on a 2009 survey, courses on instruction are offered by all but one of the library and information science programs accredited by the

American Library Association (ALA) (Roy, 2011: 274). This is a dramatic increase from the figure cited in a study conducted in 2000, when just over half of the institutions surveyed offered a course in instruction (Albrecht and Baron, 2002: 80), and it trumps what happens in most subject specialties. Depending on program track, however, instruction courses still remain elective, by and large. Even programs mandating coursework in instruction only require a minimum of one course to fulfill the requisite.

So how do library professionals learn how to teach? The majority of respondents in the 2000 study (84 percent) reported that they learned to teach through on-the-job training (ibid.: 85). It is reasonable to conclude that, like other academics, librarians were (and are) being trained by fellow librarians, who themselves very likely have no formal preparation in the practice of teaching.

Teaching styles

In conversations with fellow librarians over the course of my career on the subject of teaching, the comment I have heard most often is that their teaching style models how they were taught, and how they like to learn – through the lecture. For librarians, this lecture model translates to librarian-centered, online database demonstration. In a 2002 report, this type of instruction was used in nearly 85 percent of all cases (Dalyrmple, 2002: 271). Of course, librarians are required in some instances to demonstrate the tools, or resources, students need to learn and use. Information literacy, however, requires students to learn more than just mere mechanics.

There are numerous teaching-style models. The two most general, simplistic models are:

- teacher centered (sage on the stage)
- student centered (guide on the side)

(Behar-Horenstein and Morgan, 1995)

More detailed models include Anthony Grasha's five potential approaches (Grasha, 1996):

- Expert
- Formal authority
- Personal model
- Facilitator
- Delegator

Mosston and Ashworth (1986) provide an even more detailed model (*http://edutechwiki.unige.ch/en/Teaching_style*):

1. Style A Command – teacher makes all decisions.
2. Style B Practice – students carry out teacher-prescribed tasks.
3. Style C Reciprocal – students work in pairs: one performs, the other provides feedback.
4. Style D Self-check – students assess their own performance against criteria.
5. Style E Inclusion – teacher planned. Student monitors own work.
6. Style F Guided Discovery – students solve teacher-set movement problems with assistance.
7. Style G Divergent – students solve problems without assistance from the teacher.
8. Style H Individual – teacher determines content. Student plans the program.

9. Style I Learner Initiated – student plans own program. Teacher is advisor.
10. Style J Self-teaching – student takes full responsibility for the learning process.

Teaching, however, is so much more than an intellectual, theoretical exercise. It is intensely personal. There are few endeavors more demanding of our entire selves. Parker Palmer writes eloquently about teaching as being where our personal and public selves meet (Palmer, 1997, 1998). We should remember that we are unique individuals, and that none of us will ever teach in the exact same way, and nor should we. Students are able to sense genuineness, and will respond better to, and learn more from, teachers who are passionate and knowledgeable about a subject, who convey its importance and who are enthusiastic about sharing what they know with the student. There are always areas in which we can improve our instruction, however.

Learning styles

I often wonder if those of us of a "certain age" would teach in ways beyond lectures and tool demonstrations if different teaching styles had been modeled for us. We learned by lecture because there was no other choice. There is an extensive literature on learning styles, or how students prefer to learn and think. One can be overwhelmed by the number of different learning styles and cognitive theories, as well as the literature confirming, or in some cases disproving, a particular theory or model. One survey, for example, indicates that nearly 82 percent of librarians responded that they had heard of learning style theory, and of those who had, 71 percent found it to be valid or very valid (Dalrymple, 2002: 265–7). Respondents who rated learning theory as less valid or less valuable seemed to be doubtful of educational theory in general. Others indicated that students were responsible for their learning experience and should adjust to the librarian's style, as opposed to the librarian making any change in the instructional method (ibid.: 268).

Perhaps just as we tend to favor a teaching style, we also gravitate to a specific philosophy that coincides with our personal experiences and values. Rather than recount numerous styles and debate the benefits and disadvantages of each here, an understanding of the VARK and Kolb models can serve as a good, basic introduction.

VARK, designed by Neil Fleming, is an acronym for Visual, Aural, Read/Write and Kinesthetic (Fleming, 1995). These are the four ways in which students prefer to take in information and his typology consists of:

- *Visual learners*: who prefer to see (and who think in pictures, requiring visual aids such as PowerPoint, handouts, graphs) (Fleming, 1995; Kolloffel, 2012).

- *Auditory learners*: who prefer to listen (to lectures, discussions), also known as aural learners.

- *Read/Write learners*: who prefer to gather information by reading or writing.

- *Kinesthetic or tactile learners*: who learn by using the senses – touch, hearing, smell, taste and sight – moving, touching; concrete multi-sensory experiences. Sometimes these learners just use touch (Fleming, 1995; Rogers, 2009; Kolloffel, 2012).

David A. Kolb focuses on learning as a *process* and also identifies four types of learners (and see Figure 7.1):

- *Converger*: preferring abstract conceptualization and active experimentation. Good at making practical applications of ideas and at using deductive reasoning to solve problems.

- *Diverger*: preferring concrete experience and reflective observation. Imaginative, comes up with good ideas, sees things from different perspectives.

- *Assimilator*: preferring abstract conceptualization and reflective observation. Prefers theoretical models by means of inductive reasoning.

- *Accomodator*: preferring concrete experience and active experimentation. Actively engages with the world and does things instead of merely reading or thinking about them (Kolb, 1984; Bodi, 2010; Sanderson, 2011).

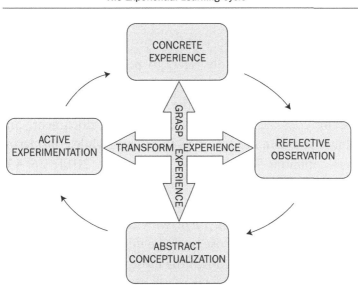

The Experiential Learning Cycle

Figure 7.1 Kolb's Experiential Learning Cycle

Source: Kolb and Kolb, 2009: 299. Reprinted by permission of Sage Publications

In planning an information literacy session then, whether using VARK or Kolb, instructors should adapt presentation styles, and incorporate active learning components, in order to meet the needs of different learners. For example, in addition to telling students the class plan and outcomes verbally, a PowerPoint slide detailing the same information will have more impact for visual learners. When crafting active learning exercises, keep in mind that students will work through assignments differently, and you may need to build in time for more reflection and thought. It is worth noting that these learning style categories are not rigid. While students may have primary preferred methods of learning, learners can adapt, and research suggests that learners are able to employ multiple styles as necessary (Bodi, 2010; Dobson, 2010; Zacharis, 2011).

Active learning

"Active learning" broadly refers to pedagogies which shift the emphasis on learning from the instructor to the students themselves. One example is the use of discussion. Students critically consider a problem, question or document, and evaluate and comment on it on their own, while considering others' opinions (Svinicki and McKeachie, 2011: 36–43). "Think-Pair-Share" is another technique where students are asked a question and placed into pairs. The pairs discuss their answers then share them with the entire class (ibid.: 194–5). Librarians also use the "one minute" paper exercise; asking students to note down the most important point they learned and what questions they still have. Debates, responses to multimedia, role-playing and gaming are other examples of active learning pedagogies (Angelo and Cross, 1993: 148–53).

Research studies indicate that active learning strategies are comparable to lectures for achieving content mastery, but superior to lectures for developing thinking and writing skills (Bonwell and Eison, 1991). Active learning by its very nature, however, requires librarians to give up a certain amount of classroom control. One can guide a session, but it is difficult to predict what students might say or do. I find this free-flowing, possibility-rich atmosphere invigorating, but some of my colleagues view the same class as pure chaos and anarchy. In other words, not everyone will be comfortable with this style of teaching. Still, consider modeling active learning components for colleagues, and encourage experimentation, emphasizing that they will not be judged on the attempt. As Palmer states, when an instructor is forced to conduct a class in a way that is antithetical to his or her identity, it will not result in a successful learning experience, for neither the teacher nor the students (Palmer, 1997). For those interested in reading about and experimenting with different teaching methods, I highly recommend *McKeachie's Teaching Tips: Strategies, Research, and Theory for College and University Teachers* (Svinicki and McKeachie, 2011).

Electronic or computer classrooms in particular lend themselves to active learning. Computer labs allow for live searching, real-world searching experiences, success, failure and experimentation. Students take control of their learning by doing. In such an environment, librarians should take care not to equate this student-centered learning with students mimicking a librarian database demonstration. Instead, the session should focus on case studies, problem solving and small-group activities and discussions, allowing students to move through the cycles of the research process in a scaffolded and logical sequence, building research skills from a basic level to more sophisticated, cogent, articulated strategies. Allow students to select their own search topics and relevant databases and allow time for peer interaction and collaboration (Gresham, 1999). At times, librarians fall into the trap of thinking that if a computer is not available, then active learning cannot take place. Nothing could be further from the truth. A whiteboard, worksheets and working on questions or strategies in groups and pairs can produce just as rich a learning environment.

One final advantage to active learning is that both librarians and students benefit from a more energized, engaged exchange. For years, librarians at my home institution conducted traditional, walk-around-the-library tours. My colleagues grew to dislike the exercise, and the students were bored. In an effort to redefine the session, we designed an "Ethnography tour," which asks students to investigate the different floors of the library in groups, create field notes and maps, take pictures and then share their findings with the other groups in the class. The class is student centered, with a librarian present to answer questions or to provide clarification. Learning outcomes include helping students identify and learn the service points within the library and combating library anxiety. Students are now actively engaged and like exploring on their own. Librarians meanwhile are now happy to conduct the sessions, and thoroughly enjoy the less formal interaction. Most importantly, the students walk away with a better sense of the facility (Noe, 2009: 22).

The classroom environment

Be careful also to consider the physical environment while planning. One often overlooked factor that influences students' ability to learn effectively is the space in which learning is to take place. Consider your own personal experience: how many early morning meetings have you struggled through, even with a strong cup of coffee? Have you ever struggled through an afternoon lecture in an overcrowded, overly warm hall while sitting in an uncomfortable chair? If the day's guest lecture was using PowerPoint, were all the lights in the room off? Do you recall an occasion when you were working on a report under a deadline, while maintenance crews were drilling on a floor below? Students are not immune to these types of environmental stressors, and the time of day, temperature of the room, lighting and noise levels all can have an effect on learning.

Bringing it all together

Learning outcomes

You now have an awareness of teaching and learning styles, have an appreciation for active learning and are mindful of the physical needs of students. How then does one begin to construct a lesson plan for an information literacy session? Debra Gilchrist provides librarians with an exemplary model, well recognized within the profession:

1. "What do you want students to be able to do?" (*Outcome*)
2. "What does the student need to know in order to do this well?" (*Curriculum*)
3. "What activity will facilitate learning?" (*Pedagogy*)
4. "How will the student demonstrate the learning?" (*Assessment*)
5. "How will I know the student has done this well?" (*Criteria*)

(Gilchrist, 2009: 73)

Begin with specific student learning outcomes. Learning outcomes or objectives are specific and measurable.

Constructing good learning outcomes is not trivial, and requires some knowledge and expertise. Too often, librarians mistake the ACRL *Information Literacy Competency Standards* as an appropriate outcome, or draft outcomes that are too broad or vague. Some examples include statements such as "Students will find books in the library" or "Students will evaluate information." I suggest using the outcomes provided by the ACRL document instead of attempting to draft one's own learning outcomes. For instance, instead of the vague "Students will use the catalog," use "Students will learn and use the Library of Congress (LC) Classification System, to locate information resources within the library or to identify specific sites for physical exploration" (ACRL, 2000: 10). This provides a much clearer sense of what students need to know (LC call numbers) in order to do something (locate information) within the library (Gilchrist, 2009). Details such as learning the LC system specifically also provide a measurable base for assessment (for more on this see Chapter 10). Educational theory suggests that no more than two or three learning outcomes can be accomplished successfully within a class session, depending on time allotted. This model works for a "one-shot" session and can be scaled to work with multiple, or semester-long, information literacy classes and courses.

In addition to the outcomes provided by the ACRL *Information Literacy Standards*, the ACRL Instruction Section has developed a document entitled *Objectives for Information Literacy Instruction: A Model Statement for Academic Librarians* (see *http://www.ala.org/acrl/standards/ objectivesinformation*). This companion document is meant to work in tandem with the *Information Literacy Competency Standards*. Use learning outcomes from either the *Standards* or the *Objectives* when developing any information literacy session.

I also recommend writing out a lesson plan prior to class, as this is a good way of organizing objectives, developing active learning exercises and timing the session. It is also an aid in monitoring progress as one teaches the class. A plethora of lesson plans are available on the Internet. Our education subject specialist, a former elementary and middle-school teacher, also developed this useful template shown in Figure 7.2.

Professor: _____   Course: _____   Prepared by: _____

Enrollment: _____   Date: _____

Goals/performance indicators	Information Literacy Standards addressed (*http://www.ala.org/ala/mgrps/divs/acrl/standards/standards.pdf*)

Outcomes	▪ Students will ... ▪ Students will ...	Materials needed
Activity	1. Introduction 2. Learning outcome 1 3. Learning outcome 2	Other resources
Assessment	Learning outcome 1 Learning outcome 2	Assessment tools
Instructor's summary of instruction	Reflective notes	

Figure 7.2   Lesson plan template from Auburn University Libraries

You now have the tools needed to begin to address the best-practice pedagogy strategy which, according to the *Characteristics*:

- supports diverse approaches to teaching and learning;
- is suitable to type of instruction (one-shot, dedicated course);
- takes into account diverse teaching and learning styles;
- incorporates and uses relevant and appropriate information technology and other media resources;
- advances learning through collaborative and experiential-learning activities;
- promotes critical thinking, reflective and recursive learning;
- builds on learners' existing knowledge, course assignments and career goals;
- contextualizes information literacy with ongoing coursework appropriate to academic program and course level;
- prepares students for independent lifelong learning.

(ACRL, 2012a)

Conclusion

I would like to highlight one final anecdote regarding pedagogy. I recently taught a class during which I asked students to answer a number of questions about a set of articles, in order to evaluate reliability, validity, accuracy, authority, timeliness and point of view or bias (ACRL, 2000: 11). Students worked in pairs to complete a worksheet.

As I circulated throughout the room, checked on progress and offered encouragement, one student posed a question which essentially asked me for the "correct" answer. Instead of giving the answer, I asked the pair to consider a couple of questions in determining their answer and moved on. A few minutes later, as I walked by again, the same student asked me the same question. As is my practice, I asked her another question in reply, hoping to lead her to her own answer. Her partner, rather exasperated at this point, turned to her classmate and said, "She's not going to tell us the answer! We have to figure this out for ourselves, let's just DO this." I thought then, as I do now, that the exchange was one of my finest teaching moments.

8

Staffing

Abstract: Staffing an information literacy instruction program can be challenging. Libraries rarely have enough personnel to conduct as many classes as they would like, much less the time to develop and implement classes. Having made the commitment to teach, however, those leading classes must be evaluated in order to help improve teaching and, ultimately, student learning. Student and teacher evaluations are important parts of an overall assessment plan.

Key words: staffing, teacher evaluation, student evaluation, peer evaluation, teacher training and development.

Librarians as teachers

There is little doubt that today's librarians are increasingly involved with, and responsible for, any number of activities directly related to teaching (Kemp, 2006; Westbrock and Fabian, 2010). Yet librarians remain reluctant to identify themselves as "teachers." The reasons are many. Some remain wedded to the traditional duties of the reference desk and collection development, and are reluctant to adapt to today's rapidly-changing library and traditional staffing models. Others juggle multiple responsibilities, and instruction may be just a part of their role. Librarians may feel that they have not received the appropriate training or earned the proper credentials to think of themselves as teachers (Walter, 2008). Perhaps we should be more confident about adopting the mantle of teacher. Students, our primary audience, do see librarians as teachers. In a study completed in 2009, 80 percent of students surveyed after attending an instruction session indicated that they perceived librarians as teachers. When asked why, students responded that the librarian *taught* them how to find information, *explained* the research process and *taught* useful and necessary skills. In addition, students indicated that librarians were helpful with assignments, answered questions and were perceived as being knowledgeable and intelligent (Polger and Okamoto, 2010). When dealing with staffing issues, then, as much as we take pride in our librarian identity, we are better served when we think about instructional staffing support as teacher staffing support.

Staffing

The *Characteristics* recommend that staff:

- are adequate in number to support the program's mission and workload; and
- includes librarians, library staff, administrators, program coordinators, instructional technologists, as well as disciplinary faculty, graphic designers, teaching/learning specialists, and other program staff as needed.

(ACRL, 2012a)

Few of us have the kind of human resources needed to maintain an information literacy program, much less grow the program. A study conducted many years ago indicated that there were four basic staffing models for meeting instruction needs:

1. Little administrative support but some of the public service staff take on the task; usually a librarian who has simply taken on the role.
2. Designated instruction positions who handle the majority of all instruction – an extremely heavy teaching load.
3. Program led by unit head and all staff participate.
4. An instruction coordinator, with broad participation by all librarians.

(Dyson, 1975)

While Dyson's study may be a bit dated, these models still seem to hold true today, and a survey of instruction programs within my home state provided evidence of all four. As expected, institutions with smaller libraries, or two-year colleges, tend to follow the first two models, and the larger four-year colleges employ all but the first model.

In many cases, we are victims of our own success. The more we demonstrate the value of library instruction classes for students, the library and the institution (Kemp, 2006), the more faculty request classes. Despite that growing demand, we can only do so much with what we have. When it comes to staffing decisions, one must think strategically, prioritize and be willing to be flexible.

First, it is important for librarians and administrators to make the case for professionals whose primary responsibilities center on teaching. In some cases, of course, teaching may be only part of the overall duties. Job searches have a way of identifying multiple needs in a library. In order to provide instruction equivalent to need, it may also be necessary to enlist para-professional staff, graduate assistants working within the library and graduate assistants in other fields of study or associated with other academic units on campus. Regardless of who teaches, however, hiring for these positions is critical.

Teacher proficiencies and hiring

According to the *Characteristics*, staff involved with information literacy:

- are knowledgeable in instruction/teaching, curriculum development and the assessment of student learning;
- endeavor to work collaboratively with others and support each other's learning development;
- exemplify and advocate for information literacy and lifelong learning.

(ACRL, 2012a)

In late 2004, the ACRL Instruction Section tasked a committee with developing a list of proficiencies needed by those who "contribute to instructional services and programs at their institutions." The resulting proficiencies detail 12 skill sets: administrative, assessment and evaluation, communication, curriculum knowledge, information literacy integration, instructional design, leadership, planning, presentation, promotion, subject expertise, and teaching skills (ACRL, 2008b; Westbrock and Fabian, 2010; see also Appendix 4). Each skill set contains core skills for instruction librarians as well as program coordinators.

I recently compared library job announcements to the job announcements for college and university teaching faculty. One take-away from this albeit rough comparison is that regular faculty announcements almost always use the word "teach" in the job announcement. Library announcements are much more circumspect, and tend to use language such as "provide information literacy instruction," "participate in library instruction," or "conduct classes." The profession would be better served if the requirement is emphatic and to the point: we need to be hiring staff who can *teach*.

In crafting job announcements for information literacy librarians, administrators should also review the ACRL proficiencies and include as many as possible in position requirements. Many of the proficiencies are already standard within a typical library job announcement, of course. For instance, under "administrative skills" one finds "works well within a team," in this instance referring to an instruction team. Similarly, other components reflect what one would require of a successful candidate for a teaching position, such as "collaborates with classroom faculty," "creates a learner-centered teaching environment by using active, collaborative, and other appropriate learning activities," and "modifies teaching methods and delivery to address different learning styles, language abilities, developmental skills, age groups, and the diverse needs of student learners." It would be absurd to include all 41 proficiencies in a job announcement, but it is possible to broadly define and communicate major requirements for teaching.

Once potential candidates have been identified, it is important that those brought in for an on-campus interview demonstrate and provide evidence exemplifying many of the proficiencies. One of the most common and preferable ways to accomplish this is by having the applicant present a sample classroom session. While it may not be possible to have the candidate conduct an actual class, faculty and staff can serve as a mock audience. Some may argue that such an exercise is an artificial construct with little value, but in fact it can offer a fairly accurate insight into a candidate's depth of information literacy knowledge, classroom organizational and presentation skills, and philosophy of teaching. The presentation may not be perfect, or the applicant may be more effective in some areas than others. But is the candidate self-aware enough to recognize the strengths and weaknesses of the demonstration? Do they have the proficiency to ask questions about the existing program's teaching philosophy and express interest in learning more about, as well as contributing to, the program? A librarian newly out of library school may not be particularly polished, but can demonstrate a genuine willingness to adapt and learn. Everyone can improve from further development and training, but the more successful candidates demonstrate a native curiosity and intelligence.

Teacher training and development

Yet classroom training will be required. As discussed previously, most of those securing degrees in library and information science have not received adequate teacher training through coursework. Librarians are well aware of this lack of training. In a recent study conducted by Westbrock and Fabian, librarians rated themselves against the proficiencies. According to the survey, those proficiencies with the highest means included:

> collaborates with classroom faculty to integrate ... into sessions, assignments and course content; assists learners to assess their information needs, differentiation among sources of information and develop information literacy skills (i.e. help students learn to find, evaluate and use sources); scales presentation content to amount of time and space available, seeks to clarify confusing terminology, plans presentation content and delivery in advance and manages preparation time.
>
> (Westbrock and Fabian, 2010: 575)

Librarians in contrast reported the lowest levels of proficiencies, including:

> represents the library and instruction program at conferences; uses the vocabulary for the subject and related disciplines in the classroom and when working with departmental faculty and students; maintains and reports stats reflecting own instruction activities, identifies core primary and secondary sources within the subject area and requests feedback from peers.
>
> (Ibid: 577–8)

Thus, respondents were keenly aware they would need to acquire proficiencies outside of library school, reporting that 37 out of 41 proficiencies would be learned on the job. Key among those proficiencies were learning styles (voice, eye contact and gesture), keeping current with basic precepts and theories, and reflecting on practice to improve teaching skills. When librarians were asked how they would like to acquire and develop these proficiencies, the results varied. There is little consensus on how librarians prefer to learn – for some proficiencies they prefer one format over another. Some prefer formal continuing education classes or learning on their own (ibid.: 585–7).

However, whether someone is fresh out of library school, or has been in the profession for some time, it is clear that teacher training and development is critical, and recognized within the *Characteristics* as follows:

- garner expertise in developing, coordinating, implementing, evaluating and revising information literacy programs;
- engage in professional development and training.

(ACRL, 2012a)

Weimer and Lenze, in 1997's *Higher Education: Handbook of Theory and Research*, suggest that there are five typical ways for teachers to learn and to improve their skills:

1. Workshops and seminars.
2. Consult with instructional designers and campus teaching experts.
3. Instructional grants – funding for teaching materials.
4. Distribution of resource materials – synopses of effective teaching practices.
5. Programs that allow collegial review and support.

Most institutions offer workshops or discussions on various aspects of teaching, from lesson planning, to classroom management, to engaging students. These workshops may be offered by a center for teaching, or conducted in-house via academic departments, or even delivered in libraries with a large and/or expert staff. Encourage all involved in teaching to attend such sessions if they take place, and if supervising, allow time for staff to do so.

The profession itself offers a number of workshops and conferences. Of note is the ACRL Immersion Program (*http://www.ala.org/acrl/issues/infolit/professactivity/iil/immersion/programs*) which offers tracks in teaching, program planning and assessment. Library conferences, at the local, regional and national level, also offer any number of opportunities for attendees to participate in workshops and attend sessions wholly focused on instruction.

In-house training requires the support of other librarians. One option is to pair librarians for peer-to-peer mentoring. For all new hires, our library has instituted a formal training plan (see Figure 8.1). While this plan typically requires two semesters, it remains in "draft" form, so we can adjust and scale for previous experience and knowledge. Not all institutions may have the luxury of working with a new librarian over the course of an academic year, of course, and the training schedule may be condensed.

First semester:

1. Observe general orientations and first-year experience classes. Note:

   a. appropriate information literacy student learning outcomes;
   b. interaction with students.

2. Observe undergraduate and graduate information literacy sessions. Note and discuss informally with colleagues:

   a. library's teaching philosophy;
   b. individual teaching philosophies;
   c. teaching styles;
   d. learning styles;
   e. student engagement;
   f. active learning;
   g. classroom handouts and other supporting materials/ web pages etc.;
   h. classroom management;
   i. classroom assessments;
   j. interaction with students.

3. Meet with Instruction Coordinator and Head of Reference and Instruction to discuss:

   a. overall impressions of instruction program;
   b. assessment/feedback; in your view, what worked and what did not;
   c. ideas for improvement;

(continued)

> d. personal teaching strengths and weaknesses;
>
> e. the best way forward.
>
> 4. Attend teacher training and development workshops, webinars, seminars, etc., as appropriate.
>
> **Second semester:**
>
> 1. Teach teaching:
>
>   a. begin with 20 percent/80 percent to end semester with 100 percent planning and teaching responsibility;
>
>   b. practice skills;
>
>   c. refine skills.
>
> 2. Develop own teaching portfolio/repertoire:
>
>   a. lesson plans;
>
>   b. classroom handouts;
>
>   c. active-learning exercises;
>
>   d. web pages.
>
> 3. Evaluation:
>
>   a. peer observation (required);
>
>   b outside observation (optional).

Figure 8.1   Teaching training plan for library faculty – Auburn University

It is also possible to provide training online. At one institution, all staff in learning resources – including para-professional staff who offered library, information technology and e-learning support – completed a mandatory online course in information literacy. The program started with an in-person workshop and then moved on to an online course management system (CMS) comprised of nine units. The program's goals were twofold: "to ensure a fundamental and substantial improvement in the comprehension of both information literacy and the functionality [of the course management system]" (Appleton, 2010: 94), so they in turn could better teach students information skills and assist with the CMS.

Teacher evaluation

Once staff are in place and are conducting sessions, the *Characteristics* emphasize the need for:

- regular evaluations about the quality of their contributions to the program and areas for improvement.

(ACRL, 2012a)

There are three standard types of evaluation: peer, student and faculty. In order to raise the value of information literacy instruction, and augment the perception that those teaching are equal to classroom faculty, I strongly urge instruction programs to evaluate instructors using the same methods that are used by regular teaching faculty. There will be resistance. No matter what the format, teaching evaluations are uncomfortable for most. No one enjoys facing close scrutiny, and much less so when it is viewed as a crucial element to job evaluation and, ultimately, to job security. All too often, faculty attempt to avoid it, worry, and become overstressed about it, or comply unhappily with the process because they do not recognize or perceive the benefits as part of professional development (Ariew and Lener, 2007). Some will echo faculty peers and say that evaluations are "popularity contests" that have no real meaning (Shortland, 2004). All methods should include formative assessment, including constructive criticism and feedback to focus improvement on teaching performance (presentation style, organization, content), as well as a summative evaluation of the overall effectiveness of the instructor (Fielden and Foster, 2010). When encouraging, or mandating, teaching evaluations, continue to emphasize that the exercise is *not* punitive, but rather is a means of identifying areas for improving teaching, which in turn will improve student learning.

Peer evaluation

Peer evaluation appears to be simple and self-explanatory; a peer observes and comments on a fellow teacher. Effective peer evaluation, however, requires thought, planning and consistency (Blackmore, 2005; Siddiqui et al., 2007; Bernstein, 2008; Chamberlain et al., 2011; Amrein-Beardsley and Popp, 2012). An excellent model of peer review was developed at San Francisco University Library in 1997, encompassing four broad areas. It uses a five-point Likert scale and includes open-ended questions, providing both the observer and the observed with clear documentation of what is expected, and what will be reported. Those four areas and the components for each are:

1. *Preparation*: communicated with instructor prior to the session to determine learning outcomes and activities; course assignment; customized session to curriculum, course assignment, faculty/student needs; planned to cover an appropriate amount of material; assessed the existing needs and understandings of the student before or at the beginning of the session.

2. *Teaching methods and organization*: stated the agenda, purpose and scope of the session during the introduction; addressed different learning styles (audio, visual,

kinesthetic); provided appropriate support material; allowed sufficient time for students to finish tasks; facilitated student participation; assessed students' understanding and progress throughout the session; concluded session by summarizing important points.

3. *Communication and classroom management*: spoke with appropriate clarity, pace, tone of voice and volume; posed questions to students throughout the session and allowed sufficient time for student answers; asked questions of students that addressed different levels of understanding; solicited questions from students, answered questions and gave helpful feedback; maintained good rapport, respected and encouraged different points of view; handled difficult situations effectively; informed students of opportunities and encouraged use of research assistance.

4. *Content*: introduced students to appropriate resources and tools, timely and up-to-date library materials; used subject-specific or topical examples; defined unfamiliar terms and concepts; covered an appropriate amount of material during the session.

(Fielden and Foster, 2010: 89–90; Chamberlain et al., 2011)

Open-ended questions ask for feedback on how the instructor addressed learning styles, what resources and concepts were covered, and the strengths and weaknesses of the session. The authors of the evaluation instrument reported that it allowed the review process to be more transparent, clearly articulated the expectations for both librarian and observer, encouraged librarians to reflect on their teaching role, increased awareness of new pedagogies, and prompted discussions of teaching (Fielden and Foster, 2010: 86).

Along with an articulated guide, there are three stages of a peer review. The first stage is the "pre-conference," which allows for discussion between the peers about which class will be observed, about the characteristics of the class, the expected learning outcomes and activities, areas on which to focus, and observer behavior (Samson and McCrea, 2008: 63; Castle, 2009: 74). The second stage is the "observation" itself, followed by the third and final stage, the "post-conference." There should be a brief post-conference immediately after the session and the observer should share his/her initial impressions. A more formal and lengthy meeting should be held within a few days of the observation (Samson and McCrea, 2008: 64).

Student evaluation

Student evaluation is another means of receiving feedback on instruction (Zerihun et al., 2012). It may also be one of the most contested methods (Alok, 2011). While there is ample literature on the topic, there is little agreement as to whether or not student evaluations are useful. Detractors argue that student evaluations are simply satisfaction surveys and do not measure student learning. They can be influenced by many factors, including grade inflation, the perceived level of difficulty of class assignments, and the gender of the instructor. Scholarship both confirms these arguments and negates them (Clayson, 2009). There is also no consensus on the design of a student instrument, and models range from three simple open-ended questions to multiple-item forms with adaptable Likert scales (Spooren et al., 2007). For those in favor of student feedback, the argument is that, "Students are the primary audience for library instruction; their impressions of its effectiveness warrant our interest" (Ragains, 1997: 164). Like Ragains, I am of the opinion that student feedback can, and does, provide valuable information. In my experience, students do comment on weaknesses, yet more often they remark on strengths, and they express gratitude for information literacy sessions; this positive feedback provides encouragement and acknowledgement of a job well done. If your institution uses a standard student feedback instrument, it would be wise to use as much of the original form as possible, and revise it to reflect library information literacy classes as necessary. Doing so adds value, emphasizing that library instructors are on a par with regular classroom teaching faculty, at least when it to comes to student evaluation.

Instructor evaluation

In Ragains' 1997 survey, just over 40 percent of respondents indicted use of faculty evaluation. These faculty feedback instruments often mimic student evaluation forms (ibid.: 166). A number of faculty feedback forms can be found on the Internet. In order to update our faculty instrument, a colleague and I are in the process of sending the tool to all faculty who have conducted information literacy library sessions in the past two years, asking them to comment directly on the questions and suggest ways to improve the form. We anticipate that their feedback will lead to a more effective form, and the collaboration signals our commitment to library teaching development and improvement.

Conclusion

There are many benefits to being a "teacher," including long-term relationships with students and awareness of the "cognitive, technological, emotional and physical roadblocks" encountered during the research process (Donnelly, 2000). We have an opportunity to see students as individuals, not just as a rather generic population. Teaching informs decisions about collection development as we see first-hand what students will use. We become more sensitive to students' questions and needs and we in turn can have a positive impact on students' perceptions and their lives (Donnelly, 2000; Polger and Okamoto, 2010).

	9

Outreach and marketing

Abstract: Marketing an information literacy program can prove challenging. Various and continual efforts must be made to promote the program. By raising awareness of the benefits of instruction, program offerings can be increased, and the value of the program can become apparent outside the walls of the library.

Key words: outreach, marketing, promotion.

Outreach and marketing

Defining your product

The literature on the outreach and marketing of library resources and services in general is excellent. Libraries have had success in marketing individual library workshops, information literacy credit-bearing classes and one-shots, all very visible components of curriculum and a library's service model. More challenging, however, is promoting an information literacy program. Traditional strategies for promoting other library initiatives should work for promoting an information literacy program. So why do libraries find this so difficult? A clue can be found in the first activity listed under "outreach" in the *Characteristics*:

- clearly define and describe the program and its value to targeted audiences, including those within and beyond the specific institution.

(ACRL, 2012a)

The very fact that we need first to define and describe just what information literacy is, and why it is important, places us at an immediate disadvantage. Think of your favorite consumer marketing campaign. In general, products do not need to be defined – everyone knows what a shoe, car, mobile phone or beverage is, why it exists, and what its value is, whether real or perceived. In the majority of cases, a need has already been established, and, as a result, companies spend time and money on developing new consumers by focusing on why their particular offering is superior to another. Even library users have a general, yet well-defined, sense of basic library resources and services, and why they are beneficial. Information literacy, however, for many constituents at least, is an unknown, or at best is not well understood. In short, program outreach may be problematic from the outset, yet it is vital for us to begin and sustain promotional efforts.

A multitude of voices

A strong web presence

A successful information literacy program therefore must employ traditional library marketing methods and communicate by every possible means. First, making information literacy readily visible via the Internet is critical. Is the link to your information literacy program a top-level link on the library's homepage? As I searched through a number of library homepages while writing this manuscript, I was astonished at the lack of either a top link or a high-level link to instruction programs. In more cases than I imagined, it took several minutes to actually locate a web page or guide related to instruction. Administrators and technical designers are quite jealous of available "real-estate" space on a library's homepage. The fact remains that if stakeholders have to hunt for a link to your program, for all intents and purposes it does not exist. Make a case to web page administrators that information literacy instruction is vital, and must hold a front-page link. If you are unable to do so, then secondary pages, not more than one click in, are an absolutely necessary second-best solution. Most secondary links refer to specific resources and services. The program must have a presence there.

Internal and external documentation

Information literacy must also be incorporated into as many library documents as possible. Mission and vision statements are also a form of marketing (Wallace, 2004: 5). These are vital communication tools which clearly state the value of information literacy across the institution. Integrate information literacy into library and campus-wide strategic documents when appropriate.

Librarians often create newsletters and brochures for their users. Subject specialists and library liaisons regularly create specific materials – both print and online – for academic departments. Encourage fellow librarians to include news on information literacy and the instruction program. Also consider creating a separate brochure specifically for the information literacy program and distribute it to faculty, program directors and administrators across the institution.

In addition, make use of Web 2.0 technology (Click and Petit, 2010), and develop, maintain and update Facebook pages, blogs and Twitter accounts. Library videos, posted on YouTube, and games that help promote library services and information literacy (Cross, 2009), also serve as visual marketing strategy.

Promotional events

Use library events to promote information literacy. The University of Salford, in the United Kingdom, created a week-long promotional event and worked with student life and academic units across campus to plan and market the event. The library hosted a special speaker, workshops and drop-in sessions to reach multiple levels of users (Barker-Mathews and Costello, 2011). While it may not be feasible to create a week-long program as the University of Salford did, one can incorporate information literacy into other library events – such as open houses, orientations, dedications of new instruction labs or commons – establishing the awareness that library is not only "place," but that library is "learning" too. Celebrate and communicate milestones, such as reaching a particular number of classes taught, or instruction faculty awards, publications or presentations.

Librarians as advocates

Instruction librarians, by virtue of what they do and with whom they interact, are perhaps the most valuable and visible asset of all (O'Clair, 2012). In addition to teaching, they also have the opportunity of informal and formal meetings with faculty and campus stakeholders. They conduct information literacy workshops and new faculty/graduate/student orientations. As departmental liaisons, they communicate with faculty in a variety of ways (Graham, 2008.) One of the most beneficial exercises in which I participated while at Immersion (ACRL offers intensive, immersive workshops to help librarians in all areas of information literacy; see *http://www.ala.org/acrl/issues/infolit/professactivity/iil/immersion/programs*) was the development of a personal "elevator" information literacy speech. Encourage information literacy instruction staff to do the following: create a 60- to 90-second speech that incorporates a personal definition of information literacy and why it is important. You never know when you may be riding the elevator, or walking to a building, with a faculty member or administrator unfamiliar with your program.

Community events

Involvement with community programs provides outreach as well as marketing outside of the institution (Thull, 2008). Possibilities include working with local senior or adult day-care programs, continuing education offerings, and boy and girl Scout troops. One of our more successful outreach and marketing endeavors is to work with area junior- and high-school students and teachers – we were often contacted by local schools as a preferred field-trip destination. We continue to encourage the interaction, but now we insist on a traditional tour (in the past there was an emphasis on all of the "cool stuff" in Special Collections); nowadays, the main element of the visits centers around classroom instruction and specific learning outcomes tailored to an actual class assignment. We also travel out to neighboring schools, and provide information literacy instruction for students at their home site, as well as information literacy seminars and workshops for their teachers as part of their ongoing training and development.

Ultimately, information literacy librarians must be open to every possible opportunity to promote information literacy. Work towards having other voices outside of the library sing its praises. A multitude of voices, from many different bodies across campus, serves as the best outreach and marketing strategy of all.

10

Program and student assessment

Abstract: To ensure that an information literacy program is actually meeting student learning objectives, a number of assessments must be conducted. Rarely welcomed by librarians, such assessments are critical to determining whether the program is effective. In addition, these assessments lead to program improvements, ultimately benefitting the student.

Key words: program assessment, student learning assessment.

Assessment

Questions and answers

After many years' experience, I can almost guarantee the following reactions to any mere mention of assessment or evaluation. First, observe the body language: arms crossed, eyes rolled, chairs pushed away from the table. This is followed quickly by verbal responses: moans, groans, muttered under-breath epithets. These are only the precursors to the full-frontal assault. Be prepared for the following:

- questioning
- fear and loathing
- defiance.

If you are responsible for overseeing assessment, your colleagues' reactions may feel very much like a personal attack. First and foremost, keep in mind that these reactions are valid. Recall your own first experiences with assessment. How many of us ever looked forward to receiving report cards or peer reviews on class work? Evaluations and assessments precipitate a certain amount of stress and anguish for most of us. Let's be honest, the majority of "assessments" we have experienced both personally and professionally over a lifetime may not be associated necessarily with warm, fuzzy, good feelings. Nonetheless, assessment is essential at the program level, and the foundation for program assessment is student learning assessment.

To minimize the negative reaction to assessment, prepare and plan for some of the resistance you will experience. Do you have clear and ready answers to the questions that will surely come?

Question 1: why do we have to "do" assessment?

The objective is to assess student learning (Knight, 2002), which in turn suggests strategies for improvement, and determines whether the overall goals of the information literacy program are being met. Debra Gilchrist's (2009) definition of assessment, delineated by four components, serves as a practical, well-articulated model:

- Knowing *what* you are doing – student learning outcomes are the basis for all library sessions and programs. They direct session content and sequencing.

- Knowing *why* you are doing it – learning outcomes are designed and "rooted in a philosophy or approach to information literacy" (ibid.: 72).

- Knowing what students are *learning* – students actually demonstrate and provide evidence of what was learned.

- *Changing* because of the information gathered – thereby student learning is improved.

(Gilchrist, 2009)

When speaking with colleagues and other stakeholders, continually make reference to student learning and student learning improvement. This should become something akin to litany when discussing assessment, something reiterated time and again in order to connect assessment to its primary objective permanently. The information literacy program, the library and the institution have a vested interested in demonstrating participation, effectiveness and value in enhancing student learning (Larsen et al., 2010).

Question 2: how am I supposed to do this?

Like pedagogy, librarians have little prior knowledge about assessment; support, guidance, training and encouragement must be provided. The development of an assessment program takes time, consideration and deliberation. One of my instruction colleagues, tasked with coordinating information literacy assessment, has taken two years to implement a plan among all teaching librarians. Among other things, she has created a "Student learning assessment" LibGuide, which details all the "ingredients" that constitute the overall assessment plan (see Figure 10.1).

Also provided are detailed classroom assessments, with exact instructions on how to incorporate them into information literacy sessions. In addition, my colleague hosts an assessment workshop/share session every semester, and works with librarians individually as they integrate assessment into their classes (see Figure 10.2).

Instruction ingredients

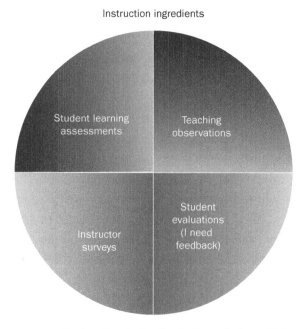

Figure 10.1 Instruction ingredients from Auburn University Libraries

Source: Toni Carter, 2012, *http://libguides.auburn.edu/content.php?pid=16741 3&sid=1410581*

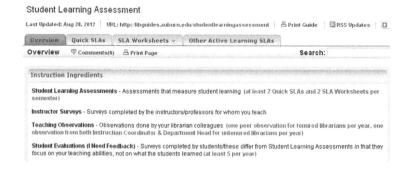

Figure 10.2 Student learning assessment LibGuide from Auburn University Libraries

Question 3: how much time is this going to take?

We have to be honest and forthright, "assessment takes time" (Gilchrist, 2009: 74). It is important to convey this fact and not mislead anyone. It is also critical that supervisors and administrators fully understand and appreciate the time involved in effective assessment (Oakleaf, 2011/2012). Assessment is not a quick, one-and-done endeavor. It must be incorporated and supported continually within job roles and responsibilities.

Question 4: how long do I have to do this for?

The appropriate response is that effective assessment is continuous and ongoing. Most librarians have an understanding of a general assessment model, and will acknowledge assessment loops or assessment cycles. There are many visual models, and the majority conceptualize the process as a continuous circle (Knight, 2002; Flynn et al., 2004; Diller and Phelps, 2008) (see Figure 10.3).

Question 5: does everyone have to do this?

Ideally, in order to maximize the benefits to students and to the information literacy program, all who teach should participate in some form of student assessment. Reality, however, may dictate a more modest involvement. The librarian leading the program must make assessment part of normal operating procedure. Allow others to witness your practice, and share your findings. Enlist others who indicate an initial interest; you may need to start with just a few people and grow the assessment program gradually. Ultimately, though, it must become standard that assessment is *not* optional, and, yes, everyone must participate at some level in the process.

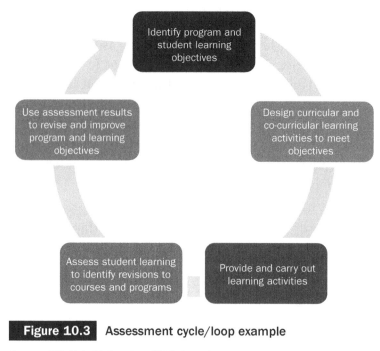

Figure 10.3 Assessment cycle/loop example

Source: CEA Global Education, 2013, *http://www.gowithcea.com/educators/global-education/assessment.html*

Question 6: how does this effect *my* evaluation?

Much like teaching evaluations and the need for assessment, the point should be made that the goal is to improve student learning. While results may be discussed during an evaluation, they should be seen in the context of faculty development and training, which will go a long way towards alleviating personal anxiety and a reluctance to participate.

Program evaluation

The *Characteristics* outline these components for program evaluation:

- develops a process for program planning, evaluation and revision;
- measures the progress of meeting the program's goals and objectives (see *Characteristics* Category 2: Goals and Objectives).

(ACRL, 2012a)

The development of an assessment plan will help guide evaluation efforts, and should be part of the overall instruction plan detailed in earlier chapters. Megan Oakleaf, a noted assessment authority, suggests that program-level plans include a statement of purpose, articulate and reference educational assessment theory, link or reference all appropriate strategic documents, list supporting organizational structures, delineate resources, detail data policies, articulate goals and objectives, and contain a timeline (Oakleaf, 2009). A survey of assessment plans available on the Internet, however, indicates that very few demonstrate such a structure. Assessment plans in practice are incredibly varied and differ in length, the amount of detail, their organization, outcomes and components emphasized. Perhaps what is most important is at least to have an assessment plan, one that can be expanded and revised as assessment is integrated into the program.

- integrates with course and curriculum assessment, institutional evaluations and regional/professional accreditation initiatives.

(ACRL, 2012a)

The impact of accreditation

The impact of institutional assessments and professional accreditation requirements for library instruction and information literacy cannot be disregarded. A 2007 survey of six regional accrediting bodies within the United States – Middle States Commission on Higher Education, New England Association of Schools and Colleges, Southern Association of Colleges and Schools, North Central Association of Colleges, North West Commission on Colleges and Universities, and Western Association of Schools and Colleges – indicated that among the six, three included the phrase "information literacy" within their standards. Two others used equivalent language (Saunders, 2007: 321; 2008: 305). One of the methods for bolstering support for information literacy program assessment is to refer to accreditation standards with administrators and colleges when discussing the need for assessment, emphasizing the necessity to institute, and collect, data well before any accreditation self-study and on-campus visit (Simmons, 1992; Ratteray, 2002; Ruediger and Jung, 2007; Larsen et al., 2010; Gustavson, 2012). Discipline-related accreditations and program reviews may also provide the opportunity and impetus to assess and improve information literacy.

Formative and summative assessments

- uses appropriate assessment/evaluation method for relevant purposes, for example formative and summative and/or short-term and longitudinal.

(ACRL, 2012a)

While there are a number of assessment methods, it is best if an array of evaluation instruments is used. The majority of the assessments most often used for information literacy include, and exemplify, formative and summative assessments.

To understand the difference between the two, consider the root and definition of each word.

> **Formative** Old French *formatif, -ive* (12th cent.), as if < Latin **formātĭv-us*, < *formāre* to form; having the faculty of forming or fashioning.

> **Summative** Old French sommer, summer (13–14th cent.), or < its source, medieval Latin summāre (whence Provençal somar, Italian sommare, Spanish sumar, Portuguese sommar), < summa sum; to find the sum or total number or amount of; to add together; to reckon or count up; to cast up (a column of figures, an account).

> (*OED* Online, 2012)

Formative assessment, then, occurs during the actual learning process, and is characterized as assessment *for* learning (Dunaway and Orblych, 2011: 26). The goal of formative assessment is to monitor student learning in order to provide ongoing feedback that can be used by instructors to improve their teaching, and by students to improve their learning. Instructors can see where students are struggling and address problems immediately. Students identify their strengths and weaknesses and target areas that need work. In addition, formative assessments are generally low-stake, which means that they have a low, or no, point value. Examples of formative assessments include asking students to: draw a concept map in class to represent their understanding of a topic; submit one or two sentences identifying the main point of a lecture; or turn in a research proposal for early feedback.

In contrast, summative assessment measures the sum of what a student has learned, usually after a particular period of time. Summative assessment is characterized as assessment *of* learning (ibid.). The goal is to evaluate student learning at the end of an instructional unit by comparing it against some standard or benchmark. Summative assessments are often high-stake, graded evaluations that contribute to a student's overall class grade. Examples include a midterm exam, final project, or paper. Information from summative assessments can be used formatively when students or faculty use it to guide their efforts and activities in subsequent courses (*http://www.cmu.edu/teaching/assessment/basics/ formative-summative.html*, accessed 25 August 2012).

Short-term assessments are aptly named and self-explanatory. They can apply to both formative and summative assessments. In contrast, the more challenging assessments are those designated as longitudinal. These assessments include evaluation over long periods of time, and usually follow the same individual. For example, an information literacy study may track a student from his/her first year until graduation. Some longitudinal studies follow groups, or cohorts, instead of particular individuals, follow a sampling of a population. Longitudinal studies are difficult to manage – the length of time required, as well as Institutional Research Board considerations for individual participants, render this type of assessment impractical for most libraries. Short-term formative and summative assessment efforts are strategic, and will provide ample evidence for assessment of an information literacy program and its students.

Student assessments

The *Characteristics* for assessing student outcomes include:

- acknowledge differences in learning and teaching styles in the outcome measures;
- employ a variety of pre- and post-instruction outcome measures; for example: needs assessment, pre-tests,

post-tests, portfolio assessment, oral defense, quizzes, essays, direct observation, anecdotal, peer and self-review, and experience;

- focus on learner performance, knowledge acquisition and attitude appraisal;
- assess the learners' process and product;
- peer and self-review meets this characteristic. Include learner-, peer- and self-evaluation.

(ACRL, 2012a)

There is a large variety of student assessment, including citation analysis, rubrics, portfolios, surveys, pre- and post-tests (Hufford, 2010) and exams (Larsen et al., 2010). These assessments can be scaled and applied at all levels (i.e., institutional, program, course and class levels) (Diller and Phelps, 2008). Some of the more popular assessments today are shaped around the concept of "authentic assessment" which simply means that the assessments are based on real-world assignments, processes and situations; real-world student work (ibid.; Oakleaf 2011/2012).

For instance, portfolio assessment is a summative, authentic method, that is, "students' selection of artifacts and self-selection of their work" and "a collection of self-selected student work and self-selection organized around specific learning goals" (Diller and Phelps, 2008: 77). A rubric can be used to evaluate these student materials (Whitehurst, 2011). Another example of authentic, summative assessment would be a citation/bibliography analysis, much like the previously discussed citation project. For authentic, formative assessments there are a number of ways to evaluate student work during the actual instruction process. These methods, also known as classroom assessment techniques (Angelo and Cross, 1993) or tools, assess particular tasks during the learning process. Undoubtedly, librarians are familiar with the "one minute paper," where students are asked a question regarding their level of understanding of a specific topic. Other popular classroom assessments include the "muddiest point" – what is the one thing not understood – and the RSQC2 (Recall, Summarize, Question, Connect, Comment) worksheet (ibid.). These, along with others, are intentionally "design tasks to assess the skills" (Mueller, 2008: 18); to ensure that students demonstrate the skills during instruction itself (Whitehurst, 2011). Classroom learning assessments and active-learning exercises often go hand-in-hand and data can be gathered, sometimes in nontraditional ways. As an example, when discussing the differences among scholarly, popular and trade publications, students detail characteristics on whiteboards. After class, we take pictures of the boards via mobile phones, and then review the content for commonalities and/or discrepancies in order to help plan and improve similar future classes.

In addition, standardized instruments are available, such as ETS's iSkills (*http://www.ets.org/iskills/about*) and Kent State's Project SAILS (*https://www.projectsails.org/AboutTest*). In my experience, data gathered from these tests is valued by those who report data at the institutional level. Such tests do come at a cost, however. Offices of Institutional Effectives or Offices of Institutional Research sometimes have funds available for purchase, as well as for personnel to administer the tool.

Assessing outcomes and critical thinking

No matter what type of student assessment is used, it is important to evaluate specific learning outcomes at differing levels of critical thinking. In 1956, Benjamin Bloom, along with a committee of prominent educators, published a report outlining a hierarchical classification of learning and learning objectives. These learning objectives are divided into three "domains": cognitive, affective and psychomotor. The committee's work suggested that within the cognitive domain students move from the lowest levels, which encompass basic knowledge and building foundational skills, to higher levels of critical thinking, exemplified by thorough and detailed analysis, synthesis and evaluation. Within the affective domain, the lowest level was designated as "receiving." At this level, students passively receive information. Bloom's group theorized that no actual learning takes place in this phase. In the higher levels of the affective domain, students begin to interact with information; they begin to attach value to information, compare and relate what has been learned, eventually incorporating information and knowledge into a personal characteristic (Bloom, 1956).

In 2000, Anderson and Krathwohl published a revised version of the earlier taxonomy, which suggested that Bloom's original noun-based construct was one-dimensional. Their revised taxonomy presented two dimensions, separating the noun-based dimension of knowledge into four categories – factual, conceptual, procedural and metacognitive – while the cognitive learning dimension was redefined as the verb-driven process (see Figure 10.4).

In 2009, Andrew Churches suggested that the Internet and emerging technologies provided opportunities for new learning and proposed a Digital Taxonomy. This "digital" narrative of learning uses the same framework as the revised taxonomy but incorporates vocabulary into each level, appropriate to Internet and Web 2.0 technologies and creative work (Churches, 2009).

Evaluation	Higher order	Creating
Synthesis		Evaluating
Analysis		Analyzing
Application		Applying
Comprehension		Understanding
Knowledge	Lower order	Remembering
Bloom's Taxonomy		**Revised taxonomy**

Figure 10.4   A comparison of Bloom's Taxonomy and the revised taxonomy

Source: Krathwohl, 2002

In practical terms, this means that assessments must aim for higher levels of knowledge and understanding. Too often, I see poorly-designed assessments which focus on the lowest level of cognition, i.e., recall or remembering. While remembering is the foundation for higher orders of thinking, this "low-hanging fruit" produces little value in terms of assessing a deeper and broader understanding of information literacy skills. For example, one of the assessment questions I see over and over again asks for students to rattle off the library homepage URL. I know that my students can locate our library's homepage from a variety of different access points, from the university's homepage to Google. While memorizing the URL is one of those "nice-to-know" items, I am much more interested in discovering if students understand what kinds of resources they can access from the homepage, how to critically select those resources and evaluate the information found therein. Assessing higher-order thinking skills is more challenging, yet I would argue that it is more valuable to both the student and the information literacy program.

Once assessments have been conducted, how does one evaluate the results? Rubrics have become a common and popular method used to rate or grade student results and products (Diller and Phelps, 2008; Warner, 2009). Rubrics are detailed standards outlining various measurable levels of accomplishment. The RAILS (Rubric Assessment of Information Literacy Skills) project (*http://railsontrack.info/*), an Institute of Museum and Library Service (IMLS)-funded research study spearheaded by Megan Oakleaf (see *http://www.imls.gov/about/default.aspx*), is an invaluable resource for rubrics, discussion and inspiration. In addition to using existing rubrics, it is also beneficial to develop or modify rubrics with the assistance of faculty, enhancing collaborative efforts via assessment (Flynn et al., 2004; Diller and Phelps, 2008; Tyron et al., 2010; Oakleaf, 2011/2012).

Once student assessment data has been collected and analyzed, and served as an impetus for change and improvement, summary assessments of the overall information literacy program may be made. Assessment is critical and serves as "the story of our students' learning, the story of our instruction program, the story of our contributions to overall student success" (Gilchrist, 2009: 74). In effect, it is a never-ending story, retold and reshaped to meet the needs of students today, and of those who follow after.

11

The road ahead

Abstract: The role of the library is changing rapidly overall. An information literacy program must be flexible and ready to adapt, aware of future trends and how they may impact the program in the future. Two important trends looming on the horizon involve distance learning and the massive open online courseware phenomenon.

Key words: future trends, massive open online courses (MOOCs), online learning, distance education.

Future trends

There is little doubt that libraries and their roles are changing at an unprecedented pace. Librarianship is a profession that historically has been able to take time to plan and manage change. After all, librarians are notorious for wanting to dot every "i" and cross every "t." The speed of the transformation of libraries in the past decade has been monumental, however. Obviously, some libraries manage better than others. Some manage with some degree of success; others are simply unable to cope, and find themselves, and their users, falling behind.

The majority of information literacy instruction programs fall somewhere in the middle of the continuum. Most of the librarians with whom I interact deal with a reality on the ground that includes: both campus and library administration expectations, directives and demands; changing, and in many cases increasing, job responsibilities; and library personnel at varying stages of their careers; all set within a current economic environment that limits or depletes budgets while coupled with an ever-increasing student population.

It is difficult to look ahead and plan for future trends, especially when it seems that the best we can do often is just get through a day. But look ahead we must. The key lies in how we view the road ahead.

First, stay informed of current trends. According to the ACRL "Top Ten Trends" these are the principal issues: "data curation, digital preservation, changes in higher education, scholarly communication, information technology, mobile environments, user behaviors and user expectations, staffing and patron e-book acquisition" (ACRL Research and Review Committee Report, 2012). Obviously, information literacy instruction programs will grapple specifically with "changes in higher education," many of which are driven by information technologies.

Massive open online courses (MOOCs)

One of the more important trends in higher education and one that is generating a great deal of "buzz" is the concept of open or universal education. Large, traditional research universities, such as the Massachusetts Institute of Technology (MIT) and the University of California, Berkeley, are placing course content online freely. MIT's OpenCourseWare Consortium (OCWC) boasts over 14 000 open courses (Bell, 2012a; Matkin, 2012: 7). Institutions such as Stanford University are also offering free-credit courses known as massive open online courses (MOOCs) (Matkin, 2012; Salerno, 2012). The open course initiative has led to debate on how best to certify these courses so that those completing them have a transferable credit, or at least some tangible acknowledgement of the academic accomplishment for transfer purposes and employer acknowledgement. Some institutions are providing certificates for completion (Bell, 2012b) while others are awarding digital badges (Young, 2012).

There are a number of factors driving the desire and need for such systems. One is the "student spiral" (Borden, 2004; Bontrager et al., 2005; Selingo, 2012). Both literally and figuratively this represents the educational path that more and more students are taking. Fewer students are beginning and ending their college careers within the same institution within a traditional, four-year time frame. Students are taking a less linear path as they move freely from school to school, often taking time away from academic studies because of family or financial concerns. A recent study of undergraduates within the Georgia higher education system, for instance, recorded that in some state institutions, transfer students make up more than half of their population, while other schools in the system are seeing double-digit increases among the number of transfer students (Diamond, 2012).

Distance education

Distance education is certainly not a new phenomenon, of course. "Back in the day," users received and returned videotaped lectures via the postal system. Technological advances then allowed for streaming videos, and then teleconferencing. Today, face-to-face interactions are commonplace via Skype or mobile phone applications (Tremblay and Wang, 2008). Institutions are virtually stretching their geographical borders, competing to reach users across the globe. The demand for distance education courses is on the rise. Libraries have long been concerned with providing library services to distance education students (ACRL, 2008a; Shell, 2010), so it is not surprising that providing library instruction to these learners is becoming more of a priority for many libraries. A survey of library position announcements over the second half of 2012 demonstrates that libraries are hiring librarians who are solely responsible for distance education and instruction design for remote learners. This is a growing challenge.

In an effort to convince ourselves that we are providing good and valuable instruction for distance education students, many libraries are responding with online tutorials and web pages. I think it best if we do not become too enamored of a particular technology or software, nor a single technological answer to all our distance information literacy needs. Constructing distance information literacy modules, constructing them well, and then assessing student learning, are demanding tasks, and require both the time and skill sets few of us possess. Whatever we do online, we must still promote quality and value, and ask hard questions about effectiveness and worth. The *Characteristics* apply to all of our instruction endeavors, whether online or in a more traditional setting. Best practices in strategic planning, administrative and institutional support, staffing, pedagogy and assessment are as pertinent in a classroom with a chalkboard as to a chat room within a course management system.

Proceed with caution

So, a word of caution: beware the provocateur, the "person who provokes a disturbance; an agitator" (*OED*, Online 2012). I appreciate those who challenge us and push us to think in new and interesting ways, and those who provoke meaningful and thoughtful discussion. The danger for an instruction program, though, is to be so overwhelmed by possibilities that seem to loom on the horizon that we become paralyzed. Bear this in mind, sometimes futurists are right; at other times they are not. This anecdote will date me. I sat for my library degree comprehensive examinations in 1982. This was also the year that John Naisbitt's bestseller *MegaTrends* was published (Naisbitt, 1982). It became quite a hit, and a must-read in many circles, notably among my library school peers after a professor mentioned it in passing as we prepared for our comps. Among the predictions was the idea that the West soon would become a paperless society. Thirty years later, there is some truth to that. Full-text online databases have replaced print indexes, email is the preferred method of written communication, and we read e-books on electronic devices. Yet our students continue to print off voluminous notes and articles. Even my most technologically advanced colleagues, professionals who routinely use word processing "track changes" functions, admit that they eventually print out a text copy as well somewhere along the editing process. Yes, things do change, and they may change more quickly than we would like, but it is important to take a measured and balanced approach to any change. In other words, change for change's sake does not always equate to good sense and strategy.

Looking ahead *will* require us to transform our information literacy programs and ourselves, however. We will develop and hone new skill sets, and we will find new collaborative partners to help us along the way. Ultimately, the road ahead is interesting – consider it a grand adventure. We may be able to see some of the twists and turns ahead, yet there will be completely unexpected surprises and even some setbacks. Whatever route we decide to take, as long as we take that road for, and with, our staff, faculty and students, the journey will be well worth it.

Appendix 1:
Characteristics of Programs of Information Literacy that Illustrate Best Practices

ACRL's information literacy framework was officially launched in January 2000. The framework consists of five standards, 22 performance indicators as well as a range of learning outcomes linked to these performance indicators to enable the students to become information literate. Full details of this framework are as follows:

Information Literacy Competency Standards for Higher Education, the Association of College and Research Libraries, a division of the American Library Association, 2000 (accessed 2012).

The *Characteristics of Programs of Information Literacy that Illustrate Best Practices: A Guideline* was approved by the ACRL Board in June 2003 and revised in January 2012. Available from: *http://www.ala.org/acrl/standards/characteristics* (accessed 2012).

Category 1: Mission

A mission statement for an information literacy program:

- includes a definition of information literacy;
- is consistent with the ACRL Information Literacy Competency Standards for Higher Education;
- aligns with the library's mission statement to correspond with the larger mission statement of the institution;
- adheres to the format of campus strategic documents;
- incorporates the institutional stakeholders, clearly reflecting their contributions and the expected benefits;
- appears in appropriate institutional documents; and
- promotes relevant lifelong learning and professional development.

Category 2: Goals and objectives

Goals and objectives for an information literacy program:

- are consistent with the mission, goals and objectives of the library and the institution;
- establish measurable outcomes for evaluation of the program;
- accommodate input from institutional stakeholders;
- clearly present the integration of information literacy across the curriculum for students' academic pursuits and effective lifelong learning (see Category 5: Articulation);
- accommodate sequential growth of students' skills and understanding throughout their education (see Category 5: Articulation); and
- take into account all learners served by or connected to the institution, regardless of delivery systems or location.

Category 3: Planning

Planning for an information literacy program:

- articulates and develops mechanisms to implement and/or adapt components of the best practices listed in this document (as needed):

  - mission
  - goals and objectives
  - administration and institutional support
  - articulation (program sequence) with the curriculum
  - collaboration
  - pedagogy
  - staffing
  - outreach
  - assessment/evaluation;

- addresses current opportunities and challenges;
- is tied to library, institutional and information technology planning and budgeting cycles;
- incorporates findings from environmental scans;
- accommodates the level of the program, department and institution;
- addresses and prioritizes human, technological and financial resources (both current and projected), taking into account administrative and institutional support;
- encourages librarian, faculty and administrator collaboration at the outset;
- enables librarians to take on leadership roles that will extend beyond the planning stages;

- includes a program for training and development (see Category 8: Staffing); and
- provides a timeline for systematic revision.

Category 4: Administrative and institutional support

Administration within an institution:

- assigns information literacy leadership and responsibilities to appropriate librarians, faculty and staff;
- incorporates information literacy in the institution's mission, strategic plan, policies and procedures;
- provides funding to establish and ensure ongoing support for:
  - teaching facilities
  - current and appropriate technologies
  - appropriate staffing levels
  - professional development opportunities;
- recognizes and encourages collaboration (see Category 6: Collaboration);
- communicates support for the program; and
- rewards individual and institutional achievement and participation in the information literacy program.

Category 5: Articulation (program sequence) within the curriculum

Articulation with the curriculum for an information literacy program:

- identifies the scope (i.e., depth and complexity) of competencies to be acquired on a disciplinary level as well as at the course level;

- sequences and integrates competencies throughout a student's academic career, progressing in sophistication;

- emphasizes learner-centered learning (see Category 7: Pedagogy);

- is formalized and widely disseminated;

- uses local governance structures to advocate for and ensure institution-wide integration into academic or vocational programs; and

- specifies programs and courses charged with implementing competencies.

Category 6: Collaboration

Collaboration in an information literacy program among disciplinary faculty, librarians, other instructors (e.g., teaching assistants), administrators and other program staff:

- fosters communication among disciplinary faculty, librarians, other instructors (e.g., teaching assistants), administrators and other staff within the institution;

- focuses on enhancing student learning and skill development for lifelong learning;

- communicates effectively with faculty, librarians, other instructors, administrators and additional staff members to gain support for the program within the academic community;

- aligns information literacy with disciplinary content;

- works within the context of the course content, and other learning experiences, to achieve information literacy outcomes; and

- takes place at different stages: planning, delivery, assessment of student learning, and evaluation and refinement of the program.

Category 7: Pedagogy

Pedagogy for an information literacy program:

- supports diverse approaches to teaching and learning;

- is suitable to the type of instruction (e.g., one-shot, dedicated course);

- takes into account diverse teaching and learning styles;

- incorporates and uses relevant and appropriate information technology and other media resources to support pedagogy;

- advances learning through collaborative and experiential-learning activities;

- promotes critical thinking, reflection and recursive learning;

- builds on learners' existing knowledge, course assignments and career goals;

- contextualizes information literacy within ongoing coursework appropriate to the academic program and course level; and

- prepares students for independent lifelong learning.

Category 8: Staffing

Staff for an information literacy program:

- includes librarians, library staff, administrators, program coordinators, instructional technologists, as well as disciplinary faculty, graphic designers, teaching/learning specialists, and other program staff as needed;

- endeavor to work collaboratively with others and support each other's learning development;

- are knowledgeable in instruction/teaching, curriculum development and assessment of student learning;

- garner expertise in developing, coordinating, implementing, evaluating and revising information literacy programs;

- exemplify and advocate for information literacy and lifelong learning;

- engage in professional development and training;

- are adequate in number to support the program's mission and workload; and

- receive regular evaluations about the quality of their contributions to the program and areas for improvement.

Category 9: Outreach

Outreach activities for an information literacy program:

- clearly define and describe the program and its value to targeted audiences, including those within and beyond the specific institution;

- market the program through the creation and distribution of publicity materials;
- identify and reach out to relevant stakeholders and support groups both within and outside of the institution;
- use a variety of communication methods, including formal and informal networks and media channels;
- provide, in collaboration with other campus professional development staff, workshops and programs that relate to information literacy; and
- contribute to information literacy's advancement by sharing information, methods and plans with peers and stakeholders both within and outside of the institution.

Category 10: Assessment/evaluation

Assessment/evaluation of information literacy includes program performance and student outcomes.

Program evaluation

- develops a process for program planning, evaluation and revision;
- measures the progress of meeting the program's goals and objectives (see Category 2: Goals and objectives);
- integrates with course and curriculum assessment, institutional evaluations and regional/professional accreditation initiatives; and
- uses appropriate assessment/evaluation method for relevant purposes; for example, formative and summative and/or short-term and longitudinal.

Student outcomes

- acknowledge differences in learning and teaching styles in the outcome measures;

- employ a variety of pre- and post-instruction outcome measures, for example: needs assessment, pre-tests, post-tests, portfolio assessment, oral defense, quizzes, essays, direct observation, anecdotal, peer and self-review, and experience;

- focus on learner performance, knowledge acquisition and attitude appraisal;

- assess the learners' process and product; and

- include learner, peer and self-evaluation.

Appendix 2:
Information Literacy Competency Standards for Higher Education

© Copyright 1997–2013 American Library Association. ACRL's information literacy framework was officially launched in January 2000. The framework consists of five standards, 22 performance indicators as well as a range of learning outcomes linked to these performance indicators to enable the students to become information literate. Full details of this framework are as follows:

Information Literacy Competency Standards for Higher Education, the Association of College and Research Libraries, a division of the American Library Association, 2000 (accessed 2012).

A PDF of this document is also available at: *http://www.ala. org/ala/acrl/acrlstandards/informationliteracycompetency. htm* (accessed 2012).

Standards, performance indicators and outcomes

Standard 1: The information literate student determines the nature and extent of the information needed

Performance indicators

1. The information literate student defines and articulates the need for information.

    Outcomes include:

    a. confers with instructors and participates in class discussions, peer workgroups and electronic discussions to identify a research topic, or other information need;

    b. develops a thesis statement and formulates questions based on the information need;

    c. explores general information sources to increase familiarity with the topic;

    d. defines or modifies the information need to achieve a manageable focus;

    e. identifies key concepts and terms that describe the information need; and

    f. recognizes that existing information can be combined with original thought, experimentation and/or analysis to produce new information.

2. The information literate student identifies a variety of types and formats of potential sources for information.

    Outcomes include:

    a. knows how information is formally and informally produced, organized and disseminated;

b. recognizes that knowledge can be organized into disciplines that influence the way information is accessed;

c. identifies the value and differences of potential resources in a variety of formats (e.g., multimedia, database, website, data set, audio or visual, book);

d. identifies the purpose and audience of potential resources (e.g., popular vs. scholarly, current vs. historical);

e. differentiates between primary and secondary sources, recognizing how their use and importance vary with each discipline; and

f. realizes that information may need to be constructed with raw data from primary sources.

3. The information literate student considers the costs and benefits of acquiring the needed information.

Outcomes include:

a. determines the availability of needed information and makes decisions on broadening the information-seeking process beyond local resources (e.g., interlibrary loan; using resources at other locations; obtaining images, videos, text, or sound);

b. considers the feasibility of acquiring a new language or skill (e.g., foreign language or discipline-based skill) in order to gather needed information and to understand its context; and

c. defines a realistic overall plan and timeline to acquire the needed information.

4. The information literate student re-evaluates the nature and extent of the information need.

Outcomes include:

a. reviews the initial information need to clarify, revise or refine the question; and

b. describes criteria used to make information decisions and choices.

Standard 2: The information literate student accesses needed information effectively and efficiently

Performance indicators

1. The information literate student selects the most appropriate investigative methods or information retrieval systems for accessing the needed information.

Outcomes include:

a. identifies appropriate investigative methods (e.g., laboratory experiment, simulation, fieldwork);

b. investigates benefits and applicability of various investigative methods;

c. investigates the scope, content and organization of information retrieval systems; and

d. selects efficient and effective approaches for accessing the information needed from the investigative method or information retrieval system.

2. The information literate student constructs and implements effectively-designed search strategies.

Outcomes include:

a. develops a research plan appropriate to the investigative method;

b. identifies key words, synonyms and related terms for the information needed;

c. selects controlled vocabulary specific to the discipline or information retrieval source;

d. constructs a search strategy using appropriate commands for the information retrieval system selected (e.g., Boolean operators, truncation and proximity for search engines; internal organizers such as indexes for books);

e. implements the search strategy in various information retrieval systems using different user interfaces and search engines, with different command languages, protocols and search parameters; and

f. implements the search using investigative protocols appropriate to the discipline.

3. The information literate student retrieves information online or in person using a variety of methods.

    Outcomes include:

a. uses various search systems to retrieve information in a variety of formats;

b. uses various classification schemes and other systems (e.g., call number systems or indexes) to locate information resources within the library or to identify specific sites for physical exploration;

c. uses specialized online or in-person services available at the institution to retrieve information needed (e.g., interlibrary loan/document delivery, professional associations, institutional research offices, community resources, experts and practitioners); and

d. uses surveys, letters, interviews and other forms of inquiry to retrieve primary information.

4. The information literate student refines the search strategy if necessary.

   Outcomes include:

   a. assesses the quantity, quality and relevance of the search results to determine whether alternative information retrieval systems or investigative methods should be utilized;

   b. identifies gaps in the information retrieved and determines if the search strategy should be revised; and

   c. repeats the search using the revised strategy as necessary.

5. The information literate student extracts, records and manages the information and its sources.

   Outcomes include:

   a. selects among various technologies the most appropriate one for the task of extracting the needed information (e.g., copy/paste software functions, photocopier, scanner, audio or visual equipment, or exploratory instruments);

   b. creates a system for organizing the information;

   c. differentiates between the types of sources cited and understands the elements and correct syntax of a citation for a wide range of resources;

   d. records all pertinent citation information for future reference; and

   e. uses various technologies to manage the information selected and organized.

Standard 3: The information literate student evaluates information and its sources critically and incorporates selected information into his or her knowledge base and value system

Performance indicators

1. The information literate student summarizes the main ideas to be extracted from the information gathered.

    Outcomes include:

    a. reads the text and selects main ideas;

    b. restates textual concepts in his/her own words and selects data accurately; and

    c. identifies verbatim material that can be then appropriately quoted.

2. The information literate student articulates and applies initial criteria for evaluating both the information and its sources.

    Outcomes include:

    a. examines and compares information from various sources in order to evaluate reliability, validity, accuracy, authority, timeliness and point of view or bias;

    b. analyzes the structure and logic of supporting arguments or methods;

    c. recognizes prejudice, deception or manipulation; and

    d. recognizes the cultural, physical or other context within which the information was created, and understands the impact of context on interpreting the information.

3. The information literate student synthesizes main ideas to construct new concepts.

   Outcomes include:

   a. recognizes interrelationships among concepts and combines them into potentially useful primary statements with supporting evidence;

   b. extends initial synthesis, when possible, at a higher level of abstraction to construct new hypotheses that may require additional information; and

   c. utilizes computer and other technologies (e.g., spreadsheets, databases, multimedia and audio or visual equipment) for studying the interaction of ideas and other phenomena.

4. The information literate student compares new knowledge with prior knowledge to determine the value added, contradictions or other unique characteristics of the information.

   Outcomes include:

   a. determines whether information satisfies the research or other information need;

   b. uses consciously selected criteria to determine whether the information contradicts or verifies information used from other sources;

   c. draws conclusions based upon information gathered;

   d. tests theories with discipline-appropriate techniques (e.g., simulators, experiments);

   e. determines probable accuracy by questioning the source of the data, the limitations of the information gathering tools or strategies and the reasonableness of the conclusions;

f.   integrates new information with previous information or knowledge; and

g.   selects information that provides evidence for the topic.

5.   The information literate student determines whether the new knowledge has an impact on the individual's value system and takes steps to reconcile differences.

Outcomes include:

a.   investigates differing viewpoints encountered in the literature; and

b.   determines whether to incorporate or reject viewpoints encountered.

6.   The information literate student validates understanding and interpretation of the information through discourse with other individuals, subject-area experts and/or practitioners.

Outcomes include:

a   participates in classroom and other discussions;

b.   participates in class-sponsored electronic communication forums designed to encourage discourse on the topic (e.g., email, bulletin boards, chat rooms); and

c.   seeks expert opinion through a variety of mechanisms (e.g., interviews, email, listservs).

7.   The information literate student determines whether the initial query should be revised.

Outcomes include:

a.   determines if original information need has been satisfied or if additional information is needed;

    b. reviews search strategy and incorporates additional concepts as necessary; and

    c. reviews information retrieval sources used and expands to include others as needed.

Standard 4: The information literate student, individually or as a member of a group, uses information effectively to accomplish a specific purpose

Performance indicators

1. The information literate student applies new and prior information to the planning and creation of a particular product or performance.

   Outcomes include:

   a. organizes the content in a manner that supports the purposes and format of the product or performance (e.g., outlines, drafts, storyboards);

   b. articulates knowledge and skills transferred from prior experiences to planning and creating the product or performance;

   c. integrates the new and prior information, including quotations and paraphrasings, in a manner that supports the purposes of the product or performance; and

   d. manipulates digital text, images and data, as needed, transferring them from their original locations and formats to a new context.

2. The information literate student revises the development process for the product or performance.

   Outcomes include:

a. maintains a journal or log of activities related to the information seeking, evaluating and communicating process; and

b. reflects on past successes, failures and alternative strategies.

3. The information literate student communicates the product or performance effectively to others.

Outcomes include:

a. chooses a communication medium and format that best supports the purposes of the product or performance and the intended audience;

b. uses a range of information technology applications in creating the product or performance;

c. incorporates principles of design and communication; and

d. communicates clearly and with a style that supports the purposes of the intended audience.

Standard 5: The information literate student understands many of the economic, legal and social issues surrounding the use of information and accesses and uses information ethically and legally

Performance indicators:

1. The information literate student understands many of the ethical, legal and socio-economic issues surrounding information and information technology.

Outcomes include:

a. identifies and discusses issues related to privacy and security in both the print and electronic environments;

b. identifies and discusses issues related to free vs. fee-based access to information;

c. identifies and discusses issues related to censorship and freedom of speech; and

d. demonstrates an understanding of intellectual property, copyright and fair use of copyrighted material.

2. The information literate student follows laws, regulations, institutional policies and etiquette related to the access and use of information resources.

Outcomes include:

a. participates in electronic discussions following accepted practices (e.g., "netiquette");

b. uses approved passwords and other forms of ID for access to information resources;

c. complies with institutional policies on access to information resources;

d. preserves the integrity of information resources, equipment, systems and facilities;

e. legally obtains, stores and disseminates text, data, images or sounds;

f. demonstrates an understanding of what constitutes plagiarism and does not represent work attributable to others as his/her own; and

g. demonstrates an understanding of institutional policies related to human subjects research.

3. The information literate student acknowledges the use of information sources in communicating the product or performance.

   Outcomes include:

   a. selects an appropriate documentation style and uses it consistently to cite sources; and

   b. posts permission granted notices, as needed, for copyrighted material.

Appendix 3:
Objectives for Information Literacy Instruction: A Model Statement for Academic Librarians

ACRL's information literacy framework was officially launched in January 2000. The framework consists of five standards, 22 performance indicators as well as a range of learning outcomes linked to these performance indicators to enable the students to become information literate. Full details of this framework are as follows:

Information Literacy Competency Standards for Higher Education, the Association of College and Research Libraries, a division of the American Library Association, 2000 (accessed 2012).

The *Objectives for Information Literacy Instruction: A Model Statement for Academic Librarians* was approved by the ACRL Board in January 2001. Available from: *http://www.ala.org/acrl/standards/objectivesinformation* (accessed 2012).

Competency standard 1: the information literate student determines the extent of the information needed

Performance indicator 1: the information literate student defines and articulates the need for information

Outcomes include:

1.1.c. Explores general information sources to increase familiarity with the topic:
- describes the difference between general and subject-specific information sources;
- demonstrates when it is appropriate to use a general and subject-specific information source (e.g., to provide an overview, to give ideas on terminology).

1.1.d. Defines or modifies the information need to achieve a manageable focus:
- identifies an initial question that might be too broad or narrow, as well as one that is probably manageable;
- explains his/her reasoning regarding the manageability of a topic with reference to available information sources;
- narrows a broad topic and broadens a narrow one by modifying the scope or direction of the question;
- demonstrates an understanding of how the desired end product (i.e., the required depth of

investigation and analysis) will play a role in determining the need for information;

- uses background information sources effectively to gain an initial understanding of the topic;

- consults with the course instructor and librarians to develop a manageable focus for the topic.

1.1.e. Identifies key concepts and terms that describe the information need:

- lists terms that may be useful for locating information on a topic;

- identifies and uses appropriate general or subject-specific sources to discover terminology related to an information need;

- decides when a research topic has multiple facets or may need to be put into a broader context;

- identifies more specific concepts that comprise a research topic.

Competency standard 1

Performance indicator 2: the information literate student identifies a variety of types and formats of potential sources for information

Outcomes include:

1.2.a. Knows how information is formally and informally produced, organized and disseminated:

- describes the publication cycle appropriate to the discipline of a research topic;

      – defines the "invisible college" (e.g., personal contacts or listservs specific to a discipline or subject) and describes its value.

1.2.b. Recognizes that knowledge can be organized into disciplines that influence the way information is accessed:

      – names the three major disciplines of knowledge (humanities, social sciences, sciences) and some subject fields that comprise each discipline;

      – finds sources that provide relevant subject field- and discipline-related terminology;

      – uses relevant subject- and discipline-related terminology in the information research process;

      – describes how the publication cycle in a particular discipline or subject field affects the researcher's access to information.

1.2.c. Identifies the value and differences of potential resources in a variety of formats (e.g., multimedia, database, website, data set, audio or visual, book):

      – identifies various formats in which information is available;

      – demonstrates how the format in which information appears may affect its usefulness for a particular information need.

1.2.d. Identifies the purpose and audience of potential resources (e.g., popular vs. scholarly, current vs. historical):

      – distinguishes characteristics of information provided for different audiences;

      – identifies the intent or purpose of an information source (this may require use of additional sources in order to develop an appropriate context).

1.2.e. Differentiates between primary and secondary sources, recognizing how their use and importance vary with each discipline:

- describes how various fields of study define primary and secondary sources differently;

- identifies characteristics of information that make an item a primary or secondary source in a given field.

Competency standard 1

Performance indicator 3: the information literate student considers the costs and benefits of acquiring the needed information

Outcomes include:

1.3.a. Determines the availability of needed information and makes decisions on broadening the information seeking process beyond local resources (e.g., interlibrary loan; using resources at other locations; obtaining images, videos, text or sound):

- determines if material is available immediately;

- uses available services appropriately to obtain desired materials or alternative sources.

1.3.c. Defines a realistic overall plan and timeline to acquire the needed information:

- searches for and gathers information based on an informal, flexible plan;

- demonstrates a general knowledge of how to obtain information that is not available immediately;

- acts appropriately to obtain information within the time frame required.

Competency standard 1

Performance indicator 4: the information literate student re-evaluates the nature and extent of the information need

Outcomes include:

1.4.a. Reviews the initial information need to clarify, revise or refine the question:

- identifies a research topic that may require revision, based on the amount of information found (or not found);

- identifies a topic that may need to be modified, based on the content of information found;

- decides when it is and is not necessary to abandon a topic depending on the success (or failure) of an initial search for information.

1.4.b. Describes criteria used to make information decisions and choices:

- demonstrates how the intended audience influences information choices;

- demonstrates how the desired end product influences information choices (e.g., that visual aids or audio or visual material may be needed for an oral presentation);

- lists various criteria, such as currency, which influence information choices. (See also 2.4. and 3.2.)

Competency standard 2: the information literate student accesses needed information effectively and efficiently

Performance indicator 1: the information literate student selects the most appropriate investigative methods or information retrieval systems for accessing the needed information

Outcomes include:

2.1.c. Investigates the scope, content and organization of information retrieval systems:

- describes the structure and components of the system or tool being used, regardless of format (e.g., index, thesaurus, type of information retrieved by the system);

- identifies the source of help within a given information retrieval system and uses it effectively;

- identifies what types of information are contained in a particular system (e.g., all branch libraries are included in the catalog; not all databases are full text; catalogs, periodical databases and websites may be included in a gateway);

- distinguishes among indexes, online databases and collections of online databases, as well as gateways to different databases and collections;

- selects appropriate tools (e.g., indexes, online databases) for research on a particular topic;

- identifies the differences between freely available Internet search tools and subscription- or fee-based databases;
- identifies and uses search language and protocols (e.g., Boolean, adjacency) appropriate to the retrieval system;
- determines the period of time covered by a particular source;
- identifies the types of sources that are indexed in a particular database or index (e.g., an index that covers newspapers or popular periodicals vs. a more specialized index to find scholarly literature);
- demonstrates when it is appropriate to use a single tool (e.g., using only a periodical index when only periodical articles are required);
- distinguishes between full-text and bibliographic databases.

2.1.d. Selects efficient and effective approaches for accessing the information needed from the investigative method or information retrieval system:

- selects appropriate information sources (i.e., primary, secondary or tertiary sources) and determines their relevance for the current information need;
- determines appropriate means for recording or saving the desired information (e.g., printing, saving to disc, photocopying, taking notes);
- analyzes and interprets the information collected using a growing awareness of key terms and concepts to decide whether to search for additional information or to identify more accurately when the information need has been met.

Competency standard 2

Performance indicator 2: the information literate student constructs and implements effectively-designed search strategies

Outcomes include:

2.2.a. Develops a research plan appropriate to the investigative method:

- describes a general process for searching for information;

- describes when different types of information (e.g., primary/secondary, background/specific) may be suitable for different purposes;

- gathers and evaluates information and appropriately modifies the research plan as new insights are gained.

2.2.b. Identifies key words, synonyms and related terms for the information needed:

- identifies key words or phrases that represent a topic in general sources (e.g., library catalog, periodical index, online source) and in subject-specific sources;

- demonstrates an understanding that different terminology may be used in general sources and subject-specific sources;

- identifies alternate terminology, including synonyms, broader or narrower words and phrases that describe a topic;

- identifies key words that describe an information source (e.g., book, journal article, magazine article, website).

2.2.c. Selects controlled vocabulary specific to the discipline or information retrieval source:

- uses background sources (e.g., encyclopedias, handbooks, dictionaries, thesauri, textbooks) to identify discipline-specific terminology that describes a given topic;

- explains what controlled vocabulary is and why it is used;

- identifies search terms likely to be useful for a research topic in relevant controlled vocabulary lists;

- identifies when and where controlled vocabulary is used in a bibliographic record, and then successfully searches for additional information using that vocabulary.

2.2.d. Constructs a search strategy using appropriate commands for the information retrieval system selected (e.g., Boolean operators, truncation and proximity for search engines; internal organizers such as indexes for books):

- demonstrates when it is appropriate to search a particular field (e.g., title, author, subject);

- demonstrates an understanding of the concept of Boolean logic and constructs a search statement using Boolean operators;

- demonstrates an understanding of the concept of proximity searching and constructs a search statement using proximity operators;

- demonstrates an understanding of the concept of nesting and constructs a search using nested words or phrases;

– demonstrates and understanding of the concept of browsing and uses an index that allows it;

– demonstrates an understanding of the concept of key word searching and uses it appropriately and effectively;

– demonstrates an understanding of the concept of truncation and uses it appropriately and effectively.

2.2.e. Implements the search strategy in various information retrieval systems using different user interfaces and search engines, with different command languages, protocols and search parameters:

– uses help screens and other user aids to understand the particular search structures and commands of an information retrieval system;

– demonstrates an awareness of the fact that there may be separate interfaces for basic and advanced searching in retrieval systems;

– narrows or broadens questions and search terms to retrieve the appropriate quantity of information, using search techniques such as Boolean logic, limiting and field searching;

– identifies and selects key words and phrases to use when searching each source, recognizing that different sources may use different terminology for similar concepts;

– formulates and executes search strategies to match information needs with available resources;

– describes differences in searching for bibliographic records, abstracts or full text in information sources.

2.2.f. Implements the search using investigative protocols appropriate to the discipline:

- locates major print bibliographic and reference sources appropriate to the discipline of a research topic;

- locates and uses a specialized dictionary, encyclopedia, bibliography or other common reference tool in print format for a given topic;

- demonstrates an understanding of the fact that items may be grouped together by subject in order to facilitate browsing;

- uses effectively the organizational structure of a typical book (e.g., indexes, tables of contents, user's instructions, legends, cross-references) in order to locate pertinent information in it.

Competency standard 2

Performance indicator 3: the information literate student retrieves information online or in person using a variety of methods

Outcomes include:

2.3.a. Uses various search systems to retrieve information in a variety of formats:

- describes some materials that are not available online or in digitized formats and must be accessed in print or other formats (e.g., microform, video, audio);

- identifies research sources, regardless of format, that are appropriate to a particular discipline or research need;

- recognizes the format of an information source (e.g., book, chapter in a book, periodical article) from its citation (see also 2.3.b.);

- uses different research sources (e.g., catalogs and indexes) to find different types of information (e.g., books and periodical articles);

- describes search functionality common to most databases regardless of differences in the search interface (e.g., Boolean logic capability, field structure, key word searching, relevancy ranking);

- uses effectively the organizational structure and access points of print research sources (e.g., indexes, bibliographies) to retrieve pertinent information from those sources.

2.3.b. Uses various classification schemes and other systems (e.g., call number systems or indexes) to locate information resources within the library or to identify specific sites for physical exploration:

- uses call number systems effectively (e.g., demonstrates how a call number assists in locating the corresponding item in the library);

- explains the difference between the library catalog and a periodical index;

- describes the different scopes of coverage found in different periodical indexes;

- distinguishes among citations to identify various types of materials (e.g., books, periodical articles, essays in anthologies) (see also 2.3.a.).

2.3.c. Uses specialized online or in-person services available at the institution to retrieve information needed (e.g., interlibrary loan/document delivery, professional associations, institutional research offices, community resources, experts and practitioners):

- retrieves a document in print or electronic form;
- describes various retrieval methods for information not available locally;
- identifies the appropriate service point or resource for the particular information need;
- initiates an interlibrary loan request by filling out and submitting a form either online or in person;
- uses the website of an institution, library, organization or community to locate information about specific services.

Competency standard 2

Performance indicator 4: the information literate student refines the search strategy if necessary

Outcomes include:

2.4.a. Assesses the quantity, quality and relevance of the search results to determine whether alternative information retrieval systems or investigative methods should be utilized:

- determines if the quantity of citations retrieved is adequate, too extensive or insufficient for the information need;

- evaluates the quality of the information retrieved using criteria such as authorship, point of view/ bias, date written, citations, etc.;

- assesses the relevance of information found by examining elements of the citation such as title, abstract, subject headings, source and date of publication;

- determines the relevance of an item to the information need in terms of its depth of coverage, language and time frame.

Competency standard 2

Performance indicator 5: the information literate student extracts, records and manages the information and its sources

Outcomes include:

2.5.c. Differentiates between the types of sources cited and understands the elements and correct syntax of a citation for a wide range of sources:

- identifies different types of information sources cited in a research tool;

- determines whether or not a cited item is available locally and, if so, can locate it;

- demonstrates an understanding that different disciplines may use different citation styles.

Competency standard 3: the information literate student evaluates information and its sources critically and incorporates selected information into his or her knowledge base and value system

Performance indicator 2: the information literate student articulates and applies initial criteria for evaluating both the information and its sources

Outcomes include:

3.2.a. Examines and compares information from various sources in order to evaluate reliability, validity, accuracy, authority, timeliness and point of view or bias:

- locates and examines critical reviews of information sources using available resources and technologies;

- investigates an author's qualifications and reputation through reviews or biographical sources;

- investigates validity and accuracy by consulting sources identified through bibliographic references;

- investigates qualifications and reputation of the publisher or issuing agency by consulting other information resources (see also 3.4.e.);

- determines when the information was published (or knows where to look for a source's publication date);

- recognizes the importance of timeliness or date of publication to the value of the source;

- determines if the information retrieved is sufficiently current for the information need;

- demonstrates an understanding that other sources may provide additional information to either confirm or question point of view or bias.

3.2.c. Recognizes prejudice, deception or manipulation:

- demonstrates an understanding that information in any format reflects an author's, sponsor's and/ or publisher's point of view;

- demonstrates an understanding that some information and information sources may present a one-sided view and may express opinions rather than facts;

- demonstrates an understanding that some information and sources may be designed to trigger emotions, conjure stereotypes or promote support for a particular viewpoint or group;

- applies evaluative criteria to information and its source (e.g., author's expertise, currency, accuracy, point of view, type of publication or information, sponsorship);

- searches for independent verification or corroboration of the accuracy and completeness of the data or representation of facts presented in an information source.

3.2.d. Recognizes the cultural, physical or other context within which the information was created and understands the impact of context on interpreting the information:

- describes how the age of a source or the qualities characteristic of the time in which it was created may impact its value;

- describes how the purpose for which information was created affects its usefulness;

- describes how cultural, geographic or temporal contexts may unintentionally bias information.

Competency standard 3

Performance indicator 4: the information literate student compares new knowledge with prior knowledge to determine the value added, contradictions or other unique characteristics of the information

Outcomes include:

3.4.e. Determines probable accuracy by questioning the source of the data, the limitations of the information gathering tools or strategies and the reasonableness of the conclusions:

- describes how the reputation of the publisher affects the quality of the information source (see also 3.2.a.);

- determines when a single search strategy may not fit a topic precisely enough to retrieve sufficient relevant information;

- determines when some topics may be too recent to be covered by some standard tools (e.g., a periodicals' index) and when information on the topic retrieved by less authoritative tools (e.g., a web search engine) may not be reliable;

- compares new information with own knowledge and other sources considered authoritative to determine if conclusions are reasonable.

3.4.g. Selects information that provides evidence for the topic:

- describes why not all information sources are appropriate for all purposes (e.g., ERIC is not appropriate for all topics, such as business topics; the web may not be appropriate for a local history topic);

- distinguishes among various information sources in terms of established evaluation criteria (e.g., content, authority, currency);

- applies established evaluation criteria to decide which information sources are most appropriate.

Competency standard 3

Performance indicator 7: the information literate student determines whether the initial query should be revised

Outcomes include:

3.7.b. Reviews search strategy and incorporates additional concepts as necessary:

- demonstrates how searches may be limited or expanded by modifying search terminology or logic.

3.7.c. reviews information retrieval sources used and expands to include others as needed;

- examines footnotes and bibliographies from retrieved items to locate additional sources;

- follows, retrieves and evaluates relevant online links to additional sources;

- incorporates new knowledge as elements of revised search strategy to gather additional information.

Competency standard 4: the information literate student, individually or as a member of a group, uses information effectively to accomplish a specific purpose

Objectives were not written for this standard because its performance indicators and outcomes are best addressed by the course instructor, rather than by librarians. (See the Introduction and the Competency Standards document.)

Competency standard 5: the information literate student understands many of the economic, legal and social issues surrounding the use of information and accesses and uses information ethically and legally

Performance indicator 1: the information literate student understands many of the ethical, legal and socio-economic issues surrounding information and information technology

Outcomes include:

5.1.b. Identifies and discusses issues related to free vs. fee-based access to information:
- demonstrates an understanding that not all information on the web is free, i.e., some web-based databases require users to pay a fee or to subscribe in order to retrieve full text or other content;

- demonstrates awareness that the library pays for access to databases, information tools, full-text resources, etc., and may use the web to deliver them to its clientele;

- describes how the terms of subscriptions or licenses may limit their use to a particular clientele or location;

- describes the differences between the results of a search using a general web search engine (e.g., Yahoo, Google) and a library-provided tool (e.g., web-based article index, full-text electronic journal, web-based library catalog).

Competency standard 5

Performance indicator 3: the information literate student acknowledges the use of information sources in communicating the product or performance

Outcomes include:

5.3.a. Selects an appropriate documentation style and uses it consistently to cite sources:

- describes how to use a documentation style to record bibliographic information from an item retrieved through research;

- identifies citation elements for information sources in different formats (e.g., book, article, television program, web page, interview);

- demonstrates an understanding that there are different documentation styles, published or accepted by various groups (1);

- demonstrates an understanding that the appropriate documentation style may vary by discipline (e.g., MLA for English, University of Chicago for history, APA for psychology, CBE for biology);
- describes when the format of the source cited may dictate a certain citation style;
- uses correctly and consistently the citation style appropriate to a specific discipline;
- locates information about documentation styles either in print or electronically, e.g., through the library's website;
- recognizes that consistency of citation format is important, especially if a course instructor has not required a particular style.

Appendix 4:
Association of College and Research Libraries *Standards for Proficiencies for Instruction Librarians and Coordinators*

ACRL's information literacy framework was officially launched in January 2000. The framework consists of five standards, 22 performance indicators as well as a range of learning outcomes linked to these performance indicators to enable the students to become information literate. Full details of this framework are as follows:

Information Literacy Competency Standards for Higher Education, the Association of College and Research Libraries, a division of the American Library Association, 2000 (accessed 2012).

The *Standards for Proficiencies for Instruction Librarians and Coordinators* were approved by the ACRL Board in June 2007. Available from: *http://www.ala.org/acrl/standards/ profstandards* (accessed 2012).

Proficiencies for instruction librarians

1. Administrative skills

The effective instruction librarian:

1.1. Communicates own instruction activities and goals with the instruction coordinator on a regular basis to ensure alignment with desired learning outcomes and goals and objectives of the overall instruction program.

1.2. Works well in a team environment and provides team with knowledge, skill and time to improve instructional services.

1.3. Maintains and regularly reports accurate statistics and other records reflecting own instruction activities.

The effective coordinator of instruction:

1.4. Ensures that all library instructors are aware of the desired learning outcomes and goals and objectives of the overall instruction program.

1.5. Recognizes and uses the skills of other librarians and teaching staff, assigns classes and related tasks, when relevant, to those best suited for the objectives of the class.

1.6. Represents the instructional program in the strategic planning process.

1.7. Documents the activities, effectiveness and needs of the instruction program through statistical analysis, formal reports, presentations and data analysis.

1.8. Helps create teaching environments that support the needs of the instruction program.

2. Assessment and evaluation skills

The effective instruction librarian:

2.1. Designs effective assessments of student learning and uses the data collected to guide personal teaching and professional development.

The effective coordinator of instruction:

2.2. Develops and implements iterative peer instructor assessment models in order to provide constructive feedback to librarians on teaching effectiveness. Stresses commitment to improving teaching, rather than exclusively evaluating job performance.

2.3. Assists librarians to develop programmatic assessment models that measure the incremental development of information literacy skills throughout a student's matriculation.

2.4. Identifies and analyzes factors that measure the impact of library instruction programs on library services, campus programs, academic departments and student learning.

2.5. Identifies national, regional, state, local and institution assessment and evaluation efforts and works with instruction librarians to connect them with the library's instructional efforts.

3. Communication skills

The effective instruction librarian:

3.1. Maintains awareness of communication needs of different learning styles and adjusts own communication style and methods accordingly.

3.2. Leads or facilitates discussion of controversial or unexpected issues in a skillful, non-judgmental manner that helps students to learn.

3.3. Uses common communication technologies to provide assistance to students in and outside the classroom.

3.4. Requests feedback from peers on instruction-related communication skills and uses it for self improvement.

4. Curriculum knowledge

The effective instruction librarian:

4.1. Analyzes the curriculum in assigned subject area(s) to identify courses and programs appropriate for instruction.

4.2. Keeps aware of student assignments and the role of the library in completing these assignments.

The effective coordinator of instruction:

4.3. Identifies and communicates regularly with those responsible for curriculum decisions at the institution, college or department level.

5. Information literacy integration skills

The effective instruction librarian:

5.1. Describes the role of information literacy in academia and the patrons, programs and departments they serve.

5.2. Collaborates with classroom faculty to integrate appropriate information literacy competencies, concepts and skills into library instruction sessions, assignments and course content.

5.3. Communicates with classroom faculty and administrators to collaboratively plan and implement the incremental integration of information literacy competencies and concepts within a subject discipline curriculum.

The effective coordinator of instruction:

5.4. Investigates aligning information literacy standards with the institution's program review, departmental learning objectives and/or accreditation standards.

5.5. Collaborates with institution-wide faculty development programs to support ongoing faculty training.

5.6. Encourages, guides and supports instruction librarians to collaborate with classroom faculty and administrators in the development of increased focus on information literacy – whether at the course, program, department or campus-wide level.

6. Instructional design skills

The effective instruction librarian:

6.1. Collaborates with classroom faculty by defining expectations and desired learning outcomes in order to determine appropriate information literacy proficiencies and resources to be introduced in library instruction.

6.2. Sequences information in a lesson plan to guide the instruction session, course, workshop or other instructional material.

6.3. Creates learner-centered course content and incorporates activities directly tied to learning outcomes.

6.4. Assists learners to assess their own information needs, differentiate among sources of information and help them to develop skills to effectively identify, locate and evaluate sources.

6.5. Scales presentation content to the amount of time and space available.

6.6. Designs instruction to best meet the common learning characteristics of learners, including prior knowledge and experience, motivation to learn, cognitive abilities and circumstances under which they will be learning.

6.7. Integrates appropriate technology into instruction to support experiential and collaborative learning as well as to improve student receptiveness, comprehension and retention of information.

The effective coordinator of instruction:

6.8 Identifies, encourages and supports training opportunities for librarians in instructional design and incorporating technology to support pedagogy.

7. Leadership skills

The effective instruction librarian:

7.1. Demonstrates initiative by actively seeking out instruction opportunities or instruction committee work within the library, at the institution and in regional or national organizations.

7.2. Encourages librarians and classroom faculty to participate in discussions, ask questions and to share ideas regarding instruction.

The effective coordinator of instruction:

7.3. Mentors librarians and provides constructive feedback to improve instruction.
7.4. Works effectively with the head of the library and other supervisors to promote and develop library instruction on campus.
7.5. Seeks leadership roles within the library and institution that promote library instruction initiatives.
7.6. Advocates for improving instructional services through support for training or improving skills of instruction librarians, better facilities, increased emphasis on library instruction by library administration and dedication of resources to these areas.

8. Planning skills

The effective instruction librarian:

8.1. Plans presentation content and delivery in advance, and manages preparation time for instruction.

The effective coordinator of instruction:

8.2. Seeks potential partners to create new instruction opportunities.
8.3. Anticipates growth and change when planning instructional services, and adapts plans to these changes.
8.4. Links instructional services to the mission of the institution and other campus planning documents and

relevant off-campus documents (e.g., national standards, key publications and reports).

8.5. Leads instructional staff in creating short- and long-term goals and objectives in order to continuously develop and improve instruction programs.

9. Presentation skills

The effective instruction librarian:

9.1. Makes the best possible use of voice, eye contact and gestures to keep class lively and students engaged.

9.2. Presents instructional content in diverse ways (written, oral, visual, online or using presentation software) and selects appropriate delivery methods according to class needs.

9.3. Uses classroom instructional technologies and makes smooth transitions between technological tools.

9.4. Seeks to clarify confusing terminology, avoids excessive jargon and uses vocabulary appropriate for level of students.

9.5. Practices or refines instruction content as necessary in order to achieve familiarity and confidence with planned presentation.

The effective coordinator of instruction:

9.6. Encourages librarians to experiment and take risks, to try new approaches and technologies and to share experiences and materials.

10. Promotion skills

The effective instruction librarian:

10.1. Promotes library instruction opportunities and services to new faculty, underserved departments and programs and elsewhere on campus, as relevant to instruction responsibilities and subject areas served.

10.2. Establishes and maintains a working relationship with assigned academic departments and programs in order to incorporate library instruction into the curriculum and other educational initiatives.

10.3. Represents the library and the instruction program in an effective and positive manner at local, regional and national meetings and conferences.

The effective coordinator of instruction:

10.4. Identifies relevant existing events, lobbies to be included in those events and creates new special events promoting the library instruction program.

10.5. Collaborates with graphic designers and web editors to create effective promotional materials for the print and web environments.

10.6. Establishes and maintains a working relationship with various campus-wide publications in order to promote the library and the instruction program.

10.7. Identifies and creates training opportunities for librarians in marketing and outreach basics to enable more effective collaboration with classroom faculty.

11. Subject expertise

The effective instruction librarian:

11.1. Keeps current with basic precepts, theories, methodologies and topics in assigned and related subject areas and incorporates those ideas, as relevant, when planning instruction.

11.2. Identifies core primary and secondary sources within a subject area or related disciplines and promotes the use of those resources through instruction.

11.3. Uses the vocabulary for the subject and related disciplines in the classroom and when working with departmental faculty and students.

12. Teaching skills

The effective instruction librarian:

12.1. Creates a learner-centered teaching environment by using active, collaborative and other appropriate learning activities.

12.2. Modifies teaching methods and delivery to address different learning styles, language abilities, developmental skills, age groups and the diverse needs of student learners.

12.3. Participates in constructive student–teacher exchanges by encouraging students to ask and answer questions by allowing adequate time, rephrasing questions and asking probing or engaging questions.

12.4. Modifies teaching methods to match the class style and setting.

12.5. Encourages teaching faculty during the class to participate in discussions, to link library instruction content to course content and to answer student questions.

12.6. Reflects on practice in order to improve teaching skills and acquires new knowledge of teaching methods and learning theories.

12.7. Shares teaching skills and knowledge with other instructional staff.

Bibliography

Albrecht, R. and Baron, S. (2002) The politics of pedagogy: expectations and reality for information literacy in librarianship, *Journal of Library Administration* 36(1/2): 71–96.

Alok, K. (2011) Student evaluation of teaching: an instrument and a development process, *International Journal of Teaching and Learning in Higher Education* 23(2): 226–35.

Altschuld, J.W. and Witkin, B.R. (2000) *From Needs Assessment to Action: Transforming Needs into Solution Strategies*. Thousand Oaks, CA: Sage Publications, Inc.

American Library Association Presidential Committee on Information Literacy (1989) *Final Report*. Chicago, IL: American Library Association.

Amrein-Beardsley, A. and Osborn Popp, S.E. (2012) Peer observations among faculty in a college of education: investigating the summative and formative uses of the reformed teaching observation protocol (RTOP), *Educational Assessment Evaluation and Accountability* 24: 5–24.

Anderson, L.W. and Krathwohl, D.R. (eds.) (2000) *A Taxonomy for Learning, Teaching, and Assessing: A Revision of Bloom's Taxonomy of Educational Objectives*. Boston, MA: Allen & Bacon.

Andretta, S. (2005) *Information Literacy: A Practioner's Guide*. Oxford: Chandos Publishing.

Angelo, T.A. and Cross, K.P. (1993) *Classroom Assessment Techniques*, 2nd edition. San Francisco, CA: Jossey-Bass.

Appleton, L. (2010) LolliPop for learning resources: information literacy staff training within further education, *Journal of Librarianship and Information Science* 42(3): 191–8.

Ariew, S. and Lener, E. (2007) Evaluating instruction: developing a program that supports the teaching librarian, *Research Strategies* 20: 506–15.

Arum, R. and Roksa, J. (2011) *Academically Adrift: Limited Learning on College Campuses*. Chicago, IL: University of Chicago Press.

Ashford-Rowe, K.H. and Holt, M. (2011) Emerging educational institutional decision-making matrix, *US–China Education Review* 8(3): 317–22.

Association of College and Research Libraries (ACRL) (2000) *Information Literacy Competency Standards for Higher Education*. Chicago, IL: American Library Association. Available from: *http://www.ala.org/acrl/sites/ala.org.acrl/files/content/standards/standards.pdf*.

Association of College and Research Libraries (ACRL) (2008a) *Standards for Distance Learning Library Services*. Available from: *http://www.ala.org/acrl/standards/guidelines distancelearning*.

Association of College and Research Libraries (ACRL) (2008b) *Standards for Proficiencies for Instruction Librarians and Coordinator*. Chicago, IL: American Library. Available from: *http://www.ala.org/acrl/sites/ala.org.acrl/files/content/standards/profstandards.pdf*.

Association of College and Research Libraries (ACRL) (2012a) *Characteristics of Programs of Information Literacy that Illustrate Best Practices: A Guideline.* Approved by the ACRL Board, June 2003, revised January 2012. Available from: *http://www.ala.org/acrl/standards/characteristics.*

Association of College and Research Libraries (ACRL) (September 2012b) Research planning and review committee. 2012 top ten trends in academic libraries: a review of the trends and issues affecting academic libraries, *College and Research Libraries News* 73(6): 311–20.

Atkins, S.A. (1991) *The Academic Library in the American University.* Chicago, IL: American Library Association.

Auburn University Libraries (2012) Aubie asks @ the libraries videos. Available from: *http://www.lib.auburn.edu/aubieasks/.*

Balas, J.L. (2007) Do you know what your mission is? *Computers in Libraries* 27(2): 30–2.

Barefoot, B.O. (2005) *Achieving and Sustaining Institutional Excellence for the First Year of College.* San Francisco, CA: Jossey-Bass.

Barefoot, B.O. (January 2006) Bridging the chasm: first-year students and the library, *Chronicle of Higher Education* 52(20). Available from: *http://chronicle.com/article/Bridging-the-Chasm-First-Year/20514.*

Barker-Mathews, S. and Costello, M. (2011) If the library is the heart of the university, then information literacy is the brain: promoting "Information Literacy Week" at Salford University, *SCONUL Focus* 52. Available from: *http://www.sconul.ac.uk/publications/newsletter/52/10.pdf.*

Bauerlein, M. (2008) *The Dumbest Generation: How the Digital Age Stupefies Young Americans and Jeopardizes Our Future (Or, Don't Trust Anyone Under 30).* New York: Jeremy P. Tarcher/Penguin.

Behar-Horenstein, L.S. and Morgan, R.R. (1995) Narrative research, teaching, and teacher thinking: perspectives and possibilities, *Peabody Journal of Education* 70(2): 139–61.

Behar-Horenstein, L.S., Isaac, C.A., Seabert, D.M. and Davis, C. (2006a) What happens in classrooms when instruction is not occurring: a case study, *Education and Society* 24(3): 83–100.

Behar-Horenstein, L.S., Mitchell, G.S., Notzer, N., Penfield, R. and Eli, I. (2006b) Teaching style beliefs among U.S. and Israeli faculty, *Journal of Dental Education*. Available from: *http:www.jdentaled.org/cgi/reprint/70/8/851.pdf*.

Bell, S. (2012a) Unbundling higher education, *From the Bell Tower, Library Journal* 23 February. Available from: *http://lj.libraryjournal.com/author/sbell/*.

Bell, S. (2012b) More certificates – less research, *From the Bell Tower, Library Journal* 21 June. Available from: *http://lj.libraryjournal.com/author/sbell/*.

Bernstein, D.J. (2008) Peer review and evaluation of the intellectual work of teaching, *Change* (March/April): 48–51.

Billings, J.D. (1887) *Hardtack and Coffee, or the Unwritten Story of Army Life*. Boston, MA: George M. Smith & Co.

Bissett, S.J.C. (2004) Situating the library in the first year experience course, *Community & Junior College Libraries* February: 11–22.

Blackmore, J.A. (2005) A critical evaluation of peer review via teaching observation with higher education, *International Journal of Educational Management* 19(2/3): 218–32.

Blankenship, L. and Fox, L.M. (1998) Information literacy – the next generation: evolving with the curriculum, *Colorado Libraries* 24(Winter): 21–3.

Bloom, B.S. (1956) *Taxonomy of Educational Objectives: The Classification of Education Goals*. New York: Longman's, Green & Co.

Bodemer, B.B. (2012) The importance of search as intertextual practice for undergraduate research, *College and Research Libraries* 73(4): 336–48.

Bodi, S. (2010) Learning style theory and bibliographic instruction: the quest for effective bibliographic instruction, *International Information & Library Review* 42: 137–42.

Boff, C. and Johnson, K. (2002) The library and the first-year experience course: a nationwide study, *Reference Services Review* 30(4): 277–87.

Bonner, F.A., Marbley, A.F. and Howard-Hamilton, M.F. (2011) *Diverse Millennial Students in College: Implications for Faculty and Student Affairs*. Sterling, VA: Stylus Publishing.

Bontrager, B., Clemetsen, B. and Watts, T. (2005) Enabling student swirl: a community college/university dual enrollment program, *College and University Journal* 80(4): 1–6.

Bonwell, C. and Eison, J. (1991) *Active Learning: Creating Excitement in the Classroom*, AEHE-ERIC Higher Education Report No. 1. Washington, DC: Jossey-Bass.

Borden, V.M.H. (2004) Accommodating student swirl: when traditional students are no longer the tradition, *Change* 36(2): 10–18.

Brasley, S.S. (2007) From an initiative to a program, *Public Services Quarterly* 3(1–2): 111–26.

Brevik, P. (1982) *Planning the Library Instruction Program*. Chicago, IL: American Library Association.

Brinkworth, R., McCann, B., Matthews, C. and Nordström, K. (2009) First year expectations and experiences: student and teacher perspectives, *Higher Education* 58: 157–73.

Brown, J.M. and Gaxiola, C. (2010) Why would they try? Motivation and motivating in low-stakes information skills testing, *Journal of Information Literacy* 4(2): 23–36.

Bruce, C.S. (1999) Workplace experiences of information literacy, *International Journal of Information Management* 19: 33–47.

Bundy, A. (1999) Challenging technolust: the educational responsibility of librarians. In: The Future of Libraries in Human Communication: Abstracts and Fulltext Documents of Papers and Demos Given at the [International Association of Technological University Libraries] IATUL Conference, Chania, Greece, 17–21 May, Volume 19.

Burkhardt, J.M., MacDonald, M.C. and Rathemacher, A.J. (2005) *Creating a Comprehensive Information Literacy Plan*. New York: Neal-Schuman Publishers, Inc.

Bury, S. (2011) Faculty attitudes, perceptions and experiences of information literacy: a study across multiple disciplines at York University, Canada, *Journal of Information Literacy* 51(1): 45–64.

Campbell, S. (2004) Defining information literacy in the 21st century. World Library and Information Congress: 70th IFLA General Conference and Council, 22–7 August, Buenos Aires, Argentina.

Castle, S. (2009) Peer observation and information skills teaching: feel the fear and do it anyway!: the introduction of peer observation at the University of East London, *Sconul* 45. Available from: *http://www.sconul.ac.uk/publications/newsletter/45/21.pdf*.

CEA Global Education (2013) *http://www.gowithcea.com/educators/global-education/assessment.html*.

Chamberlain, J.M., D'Artrey, M. and Rowe, D.-A. (2011) Peer observation of teaching: a decoupled process, *Active Learning in Higher Education* 12(3): 189–201.

Churches, A. (January 2009) *Bloom's Digital Taxonomy*. Available from: *http://edorigami.wikispaceaces.com*.

Clayson, D.E. (2009) Student evaluations of teaching: are they related to what students learn?: a meta-analysis and review, *Journal of Marketing Education* 31: 16–30.

Click, A. and Petit, J. (2010) Social networking and Web 2.0 in information literacy, *International Information & Library Review* 42: 137–42.

Corrall, S. (2008) Information literacy strategy development in higher education: an exploratory study, *International Journal of Information Management* 28: 26–37.

Cottrell, J.R. (2011) What are we doing here, anyway? Tying academic library goals to institutional mission, *College and Research Libraries News* 72(9): 516–20.

Cox, C.N. and Lindsay, E.B. (eds.) (2008) *Information Literacy Instruction Handbook*. Chicago, IL: American Library Association.

Cross, C. (2009) Making games seriously: creating a peer designed video game for use in library promotion and instruction, *Library Review* 58(3): 215–27.

Crowley, J.D. (1994) *Developing a Vision: Strategic Planning and the Library Media Specialist*. Westport, CT: Greenwood Press.

Curzon, S.C. and Lampert, L.D. (2007) *Proven Strategies for Building an Information Literacy Program*. New York: Neal-Schuman Publishers.

Dalrymple, C. (2002) Perceptions and practices of learning styles in library instruction, *College and Research Libraries* (May): 261–73.

D'Angelo, B.J. and Maid, B.M. (2004) Moving beyond definitions: implementing information literacy across the curriculum, *Journal of Academic Librarianship* 30(3): 212–17.

Daugherty, A. and Russo, M.F. (compilers) (2007) *Information Literacy Programs in the Digital Age:*

Educating College and University Students Online. Chicago, IL: American Library Association.

Dewey, B. (ed.) (2010) *Transforming Research Libraries for the Global Knowledge Society.* Oxford: Chandos Publishing.

Diamond, L. (September 2012) Georgia colleges transfer attention to transfer students, *Atlanta Journal-Constitution.* Available from: *http://www.ajc.com/news/news/state-regional/georgia-colleges-transfer-attention-to-transfer-st/nR2Jf/.*

Dictionary of Business (3rd edition) (2002). Oxford: Oxford University Press.

Diller, K.R. and Phelps, S.F. (2008) Learning outcomes, portfolios, and rubrics, oh my! Authentic assessment of an information literacy program, *portal: Libraries and the Academy* 8(1): 75–89.

Dillon, N. (2007) Educating Generation Z: What will the graduate of 2020 look like? Take a virtual peek into the future, *American School Board Journal* (September): 35–6.

Dobson, J.L. (2010) A comparison between learning style preferences and sex, status and course performance, *Advances in Physiology Education* 34(December): 197–204.

Donnelly, K. (2000) Reflections on what happens when librarians become teachers, *Computers in Libraries* 20(March): 46–9.

Dunaway, M.K. and Orblych, M.T. (2011) Formative assessment: transforming information literacy instruction, *Reference Services Review* 39(1): 24–41.

Durisin, P. (ed.) (2002) *Information Literacy Programs: Successes and Challenges.* New York: Haworth Information Press.

Dyson, A.J. (1975) Organizing undergraduate library instruction: the English and American experience, *Journal of Academic Librarianship* 1(1): 9–13.

Ellison, A.B. (2004) Positive faculty/librarian relationships for productive library assignments, *Community & Junior College Libraries* 12(2): 23–7.

Elmborg, J.K. (2003) Information literacy and writing across the curriculum: sharing the vision, *Reference Services Review* 31(1): 68–80.

Elmore, T. (2010) *Generation iY: Our Last Chance to Save Their Future.* Atlanta, GA: Poet Gardener Publishing.

Erazo, E. (2002) Using technology to promote information literacy in Florida's community colleges, *Florida Libraries* (Fall): 20–2.

Fahey, W., King, W.R. and Narayanan, V.K. (1981) Environmental scanning and forecasting in strategic planning – the state of the art, *Long Range Planning* 14(February): 32–9.

Fielden, N. and Foster, M. (2010) Crossing the rubricon: evaluating the information literacy instructor, *Journal of Information Literacy* 4(2): 78–90.

Fisher, P.H. and Pride, M.M. (2005) *Blueprint for your Library Marketing Plan: A Guide to Help you Survive and Thrive.* Chicago, IL: American Library Association.

Fleming, N.D. (1995) I'm different; not dumb. Modes of presentation (VARK) in the tertiary classroom. In A. Zelmer (ed.), *Proceedings of the 1995 Annual Conference of the Higher Education and Research and Development in Higher Education Development Society of Australasia* (HERDSA), *HERDSA* 18: 308–13.

Flynn, C., Gilchrist, D. and Olson, L. (2004) Using the assessment cycle as a tool for collaboration, *Resource Sharing & Information Networks* 17(1/2): 187–203.

Fox, S. and Jones, S. (July 2009) The social life of health information. Pew Report. Available from: *http://www. pewinternet.org/Reports/2009/8-The-Social-Life-of-*

Health-Information/02-A-Shifting-Landscape/1-Americans-are-tapping-into-a-widening-network-of-both-online-and-offline-sources.aspx (accessed 25 July 2012).

Frier, R., Musgrove, C. and Zahner, J. (2001) Information literacy in higher education: is there a gap? In: Annual Proceedings of Selected Research and Development [and] Practice Papers Presented at the 24th National Convention of the Association for Educational Communications and Technology, Atlanta, GA, 8–12 November 2001. Volumes 1–2.

Galvin, J. (2005) Alternative strategies for promoting information literacy, *Journal of Academic Librarianship* 31(4): 353–7.

Gavin, C. (2008) *Teaching Information Literacy: A Conceptual Approach*. Lanham, MD: Scarecrow Press, Inc.

Gibson, C. (2006) *Student Engagement and Information Literacy*. Chicago, IL: American Library Association.

Gilchrist, D.L. (2009) A twenty year path: learning about assessment; learning from assessment, *Communications in Information Literacy* 3(2): 70–9.

Glass, K.T. (2007) *Curriculum Mapping: A Step-by-Step Guide for Creating Curriculum Year Overviews*. Thousand Oaks, CA: Corwin Press.

Glitz, B. (1998) *Focus Groups for Libraries and Librarians*. Chicago, IL: Medical Library Association.

Goodson, C. (2001) *Providing Library Services for Distance Education Students: A How-To-Do-It Manual, Number 108*. New York: Neal-Schuman Publishers, Inc.

Graham, J.M. (2008) Successful liaison marketing strategies for library instruction: the proof is in the pudding, *The Southeastern Librarian* 56(1): 4–7.

Grasha, A.F. (1996) *Teaching with Style*. Pittsburgh, PA: Alliance Publishers.

Grassian, E.S. and Kaplowitz, J.R. (2005) *Learning to Lead and Manage Information Literacy Instruction.* New York: Neal-Schuman Publishers, Inc.

Grassian, E.S. and Kaplowitz, J.R. (2009) *Information Literacy Instruction: Theory and Practice*, 2nd edition. New York: Neal-Schuman Publishers, Inc.

Greenbaum, T.L. (1993) *Handbook for Focus Group Research.* New York: Lexington Books.

Gresham, K. (1999) Experiential learning theory, library instruction, and the electronic classroom, *Colorado Libraries* 25(2): 28–31.

Gross, M. and Latham, D. (2009) Undergraduate perceptions of information literacy: defining, attaining, and self-assessing skills, *College & Research Libraries* (July): 336–50.

Gustavson, A. (2012) Using ILIAC to systematically plan and implement a library information literacy assessment program for freshman classes, *Public Services Quarterly* 8: 97–113.

Hale, J.A. (2008) *A Guide to Curriculum Mapping: Planning, Implementing, and Sustaining the Process.* Thousand Oaks, CA: Corwin Press.

Haley, D., Henke, J. and Lawrence, S. (January 2006) Why study users? An environmental scan of use and users of digital resources in humanities and social sciences undergraduate education, *Research and Occasional Papers Series.* Available from: *http://escholarship.org/uc/item/61g3s91k.*

Hardesty, L. (1991) *Faculty and the Library: The Undergraduate Experience.* Norwood, NJ: Ablex Publishing Corp.

Hardesty, L. (ed.) (2007) *The Role of the Library in the First College Year.* Columbia, SC: University of South Carolina,

National Resource Center for The First-Year Experience and Students in Transition, Monograph No. 45.

Hardesty, L., Hastreiter, J. and Henderson, D. (1988) Development of college library mission statements, *Journal of Library Administration* 9(3): 11–34.

Harley, D., Henke, J. and Lawrence, S. (2006) Why study users? An environmental scan of use and users of digital resources in humanities and social sciences undergraduate education, *Research and Occasional Papers Series* (September): 1–17. Available from: *http://escholarhsip. org/uc/item/61g3s91k*.

Hauxwell, H. (2008) Information literacy at the service desk: the role of circulations staff in promoting information literacy, *Journal of Information Literacy* 2(2): 1–9.

Hayes, R.M. (1993) *Strategic Management for Academic Libraries: A Handbook*. Westport, CT: Greenwood Press.

Hensley, R.B. (2004) Getting to goals: new influences on the role of goals in active and sustainable literacy programs. In S.C. Curzon and L.D. Lampert (eds.), *Proven Strategies for Building an Information Literacy Program*. New York: Neal-Schuman Publishers, Inc.

Hernon, P. and R.E. Dugan (2002) *An Action Plan for Outcomes Assessment in Your Library*. Chicago, IL: American Library Association.

Holman, L. (2011) Millennial students' mental models of search: implications for academic librarians and database developers, *The Journal of Academic Librarianship* 37(1): 19–27.

Horn, L.J. and Carroll, C.D. (September 1998) Stopouts or stayouts? Undergraduates who leave college in their first year, National Center for Education Statistics, Statistical Analysis Report.

Howard, R.M., Rodrigue, T.K. and Serviss, T.C. (2010) Writing from sources, writing from sentences. *Writing and Pedagogy* 2(2): 177–92.

Howze, P.C. and Dalrymple, C. (2004) Consensus without all the meetings: using the Delphi method to determine course content for library instruction, *Reference Services Review* 32(2): 174–84.

Hufford, J.R. (2010) What are they learning? Pre- and post-assessment surveys for LILNR 1100, Introduction to Library Research, *College & Research Libraries* 71(2): 139–58.

Hunt, F. and Birks, J. (2004) Best practices in information literacy, *portal: Libraries and the Academy* 4(1): 27–39.

Iannuzzi, P. (1998) Faculty development and information literacy: establishing campus partnerships, *Reference Services Review* 26(3): 97–102.

Jacobs, H.L.M. and Jacobs, D. (2009) Transforming the one-shot library sessions into pedagogical collaboration: information literacy and the English composition class, *Reference & Users Services Quarterly* 49(1): 72–82.

Jacobson, T.E. and Mackey, T.P. (2007) *Information Literacy Collaborations that Work*. New York: Neal-Schuman Publishers, Inc.

Jewitt, C. (2006) *Technology, Literacy and Learning: A Multimodal Approach*. New York: Routledge.

Johnson, C.M., Lindsay, E.B. and Walker, S. (2008) Learning more about how they think: information literacy instruction in a campus-wide critical thinking project, *College & Undergraduate Libraries* 15(1/2): 231–54.

Johnson, W.G. (2009) Developing an information literacy action plan, *Community & Junior College Libraries* 15: 212–16.

Jones, S., Johnson-Yale, C., Millermaier, S. and Pérez, F.S. (2008) Academic work, the Internet and U.S. college students, *Internet and Higher Education* 11: 165–77.

Joseph, P.B., Bravmann, S.L., Windschitl, M.A., Mikel, E.R. and Green, N.S. (2000) *Cultures of Curriculum*. Mahwah, NJ: Lawrence Erlbaum Associates.

Julein, H. and Genuis, S.K. (2011) Librarians' experiences of the teaching role: a national survey of librarians, *Science Library & Information Research* 33: 103–11.

Kangas, J., Budros, K. and Yoshioka, J. (2000) Who are our students? What are our challenges? *Our Diverse Students and Their Needs: Student Demographics and Diversity Data*, ERIC Document 467455.

Karshmer, E. and Bryan, J.E. (2011) Building a first-year information literacy experience: integrating best practices in education and ACRL IL competency standards for higher education, *Journal of Academic Librarianship* 37(3): 255–66.

Keeran, P., Moulton-Gertig, S.L., Levine-Clark, M., Schlotzhauer, N., Gil, E. et al. (2007) *Research within the Disciplines: Foundations for Reference and Library Instruction*. Lanham, MD: Scarecrow Press, Inc.

Kemp, B.E., Nofsinger, M.M. and Spitzer, A.M. (1986) Building a bridge: articulation programs for bibliographic instruction, *College and Research Libraries* 47(September): 470–4.

Kemp, J. (2006) Isn't being a librarian enough? Librarians as classroom teachers, *College & Undergraduate Libraries* 13(3): 4–23.

Knight, L.A. (2002) The role of assessment in library user education, *Reference Services Review* 30(1): 15–24.

Kolb, A.Y. and Kolb, D.A. (2009) The learning way: meta-cognitive aspects of experiential learning, *Simulation & Gaming* 40(3): 297–327.

Kolb, D. (1984) *Experiential Learning: Experience as a Source of Learning and Development.* Upper Saddle River, NJ: Prentice Hall.

Kolloffel, B. (2012) Exploring the relation between visualizer-verbalizer cognitive styles and performance with visual or verbal learning material, *Computers & Education* 58: 697–706.

Koontz, C. (2006) Environmental scans: what they measure and what it may mean to your library, *Marketing Library Services* 20(3): 6–9.

Krathwohl, D. (2002) A revision of Bloom's taxonomy: an overview, *Theory and Practice* 41(2): 212–18.

Krueger, R.A. (1998a) *Developing Questions for Focus Groups, Volume 3.* Thousand Oaks, CA: Sage Publications.

Krueger, R.A. (1998b) *Moderating Focus Groups, Volume 4.* Thousand Oaks, CA: Sage Publications.

Krueger, R.A. (1998c) *Analyzing & Reporting Focus Group Results, Volume 6.* Thousand Oaks, CA: Sage Publications.

LaGuardia, C. Blake, M., Dowler, L., Farwell, L., Kent, C.M. et al. (1996) *Teaching the New Library: A How-To-Do-It Manual for Planning and Designing Instructional Programs.* New York: Neal-Schuman Publishers, Inc.

Langer, J.A. (2011) *Envisioning Knowledge: Building Literacy in the Academic Disciplines.* New York: Teacher's College Press.

Larsen, P., Izenstark, A. and Burkhardt, J. (2010) Aiming for assessment: notes from the start of an information literacy course assessment, *Communications in Information Literacy* 4(1): 61–70.

Lauring, J. and Selmer, J. (2010) Multicultural organizations: common language and group cohesiveness, *International Journal of Cross Culture Management* 10(3): 267–84.

Leavitt, L.L. (2011) 21st-century workforce initiatives: implications for information literacy instruction in academic libraries, *Education Libraries* 34(2): 15–18.

Lee, M.M. (1999) A formula for writing environmental scans for community colleges. ERIC Document 447839.

Library of Congress Subject Headings (32nd edition) (2010). Washington, DC: Library of Congress.

Little, J.J. and Tuten, J.H. (2006) Strategic planning: first steps in sharing information literacy goals with faculty across disciplines, *College & Undergraduate Libraries* 13(3): 113–23.

Liu, T. and Sun, H. (2011) Analysis of information literacy education strategies for college students majoring in science and engineering, *Modern Applied Science* 5(5): 227–31.

Lloyd, A. (2011) Trapped between a rock and a hard place: what counts as information literacy in the workplace and how is it conceptualized? *Library Trends* 60(2): 277–96.

Mackey, T.P. and Jacobson, T.E. (2011) Reframing information literacy as a metaliteracy, *College and Research Libraries* 72(1): 62–78, 137–50.

Maitaouthong, T., Tuamsuk, K. and Techamanee, Y. (2010/2011) Development of the instructional model by integrating information literacy in the class learning and teaching process, *Education for Information* 28: 137–50.

Martin, S. and Petitfils, B. (2010) Shifting the paradigm: designing and implementing an information literacy course at a Louisiana technical college, *Louisiana Libraries* 72(3): 30–2.

Matkin, G.W. (2012) The opening of higher education, *Change: The Magazine of Higher Learning* 44(3): 6–13.

Mazella, D., Heidel, L. and Ke, I. (2011) Integrating reading, information literacy, and literary studies instruction in a three-way collaboration, *Learning Assistance Review* 16(2): 41–53.

McGriff, N., Harvey II, C.A and Preddy, L.B. (2004) Collecting the data, *School Library Media Activities Monthly* 20(6): 26–9.

McKay, D. and Beck, S. (2011) Critical collaborations: an information literacy across the curriculum project, *CR&L News* (March): 161–4.

Mercer, J.L. and Woolston, S.W. (1980) Setting priorities: three techniques for better decision making, *Management Information Service* 12(9): 1–9.

Mery, Y., Newby, J. and Peng, K. (2012) Why one-shot information literacy sessions are not the future of instruction: a case for online credit courses, *College and Research Libraries* 73(4): 366–77.

Metzger, M.J., Flanagin, A.L. and Zwarun, L. (2003) College student web use, perception of information credibility, and verification behavior, *Computers & Education* 41: 271–90.

Mi, M. and Gilbert, C.M. (2007) Needs assessment: prerequisite for service excellence, *Journal of Hospital Librarianship* 7(4): 31–52.

Miller, I.R. (2010) Turning the tables: a faculty-centered approach to integrating information literacy, *Reference Services Review* 38(4): 647–62.

Millet, M.S., Donald, J. and Wilson, D.W. (2009) Information literacy across the curriculum: expanding horizons, *College & Undergraduate Libraries* 16(2–3): 180–93.

Mokhtar, I.A., Shaheen, M. and Foo, S. (2008) Teaching information literacy through learning styles: the application of Gardner's Multiple Intelligences, *Journal of Librarianship and Information Science* 40(2): 93–109; *NACE Journal* 68(3): 28–32.

Montana, P.J. and Petit, F. (2008) Motivating Generation X and Y on the job ... and preparing Z, *Journal of Business & Economics Research* 6(8): 35–40.

Morgan, D.L. (1998a) *Focus Group Guidebook, Volume 1.* Thousand Oaks, CA: Sage Publications.

Morgan, D.L. (1998b) *Planning Focus Groups, Volume 2.* Thousand Oaks, CA: Sage Publications.

Morrison, J.L. (1992) Environmental scanning. In M.A. Whitely, J.D. Porter and R.H. Fenske (eds.) *A Primer for New Institutional Researchers*, pp. 86–99. Tallahassee, FL: The Association for Institutional Research.

Mosston, M. and Ashworth, S. (1986) *Teaching Physical Education.* Columbus, OH: Merrill.

Mueller, J. (2008) Assessing skill development, *Library Media Collection* (November/December): 18–20.

Naisbitt, J. (1982) *MegaTrends.* New York: Warner Books.

National Center for Education Statistics (NCES) (2011) *Digest of Education Statistics, 2010.* NCES 2011–15, US Department of Education. Available from: *http://nces. ed.gov/surveys/.*

Nelson, S. (2001) *The New Planning for Results: A Streamlined Approach.* Chicago, IL: American Library Association.

Noe, N. (2009) Ethnographer for an hour. In R. Sittler and D. Cook (eds.), *ACRL Information Literacy Cookbook.* Chicago, IL: Association of College and Research Libraries.

Noe, N. and MacEwan, B. (2010) Partnerships and connections. In B.I. Dewey (ed.), *Transforming Research Libraries for the Global Knowledge Society.* Cambridge: Chandos/Woodhead Publishing.

Nutefall, J.E. and Gaspar, D. (2008) Raise your profile: build your program, *Public Services Quarterly* 4(2): 127–35.

Oakleaf, M. (2008) Dangers and opportunities: a conceptual map of information literacy assessment approaches, *portal: Libraries and the Academy* 8(3): 233–53.

Oakleaf, M. (2009) Writing information literacy assessment plans: a guide to best practice, *Communications in Information Literacy* 3(2): 80–9.

Oakleaf, M. (2011/2012) Staying on track with rubric assessment: five institutions investigate information literacy learning, *Peer Review/AAC&U* (Fall 2011/Winter 2012): 18–21.

Oakleaf, M., Millet, M.S. and Kraus, L. (2011) All together now: getting faculty, administrators, and staff engaged in information literacy assessment, *portal: Libraries and the Academy* 11(3): 831–52.

O'Clair, K. (2012) Sell what they're buying, *CR&L News* (April): 200–1.

OECD (2012) Education at a glance 2012: OECD indicators. OECD Publishing. Available from: *http://www.oecd.org/edu/EAG%202012_e-book_EN_200912.pdf* and *http://dx.doi.org/10.1787/eag-2012-en*.

Ovadia, S. (2010) Writing as an information literacy tool: bringing writing in the disciplines to an online library class, *Journal of Library Administration* 50: 899–908.

Owusu-Ansah, E.K. (2005) Debating definitions of information literacy: enough is enough! *Library Review* 54(6): 366–74.

Palmer, P.J. (1997) The heart of a teacher: identity and integrity in teaching, *Change Magazine* 29(6): 14–21. Available from: *http://www.couragerenewal.org/parker/writings/heart-of-a-teacher*.

Palmer, P.J. (1998) *The Courage to Teach: Exploring the Inner Landscape of a Teacher's Life*. San Francisco, CA: Jossey-Bass Publishers.

Paparone, C.R. (2010) Thinking in fours, *Defense AT & L* (February): 70–2.

Patterson, A. (2009) A needs analysis for information literacy provision for research: a case study in University College Dublin, *Journal of Information Literacy* 3(1): 5–18.

Peel, M. (2000) "Nobody cares": the challenge of isolation in school to university transition, *Australian Journal of Institutional Research* 9(1): 22–34.

Piette, M.I. (1995) Library instruction: principles, theories, connections and challenges, *Reference Librarian* 51(51): 77–88.

Pinto, M. (2012) Information literacy perceptions and behaviour among history students, *Aslib Proceedings: New Information Perspectives* 64(3): 304–27.

Polger, M.A. and Okamoto, K. (2010) Can't anyone be a teacher anyway?: student perceptions of academic librarians as teachers, *Library Philosophy and Practice* (e-journal), Paper 328: 1–16. Available from: *http:/digitalcommons.unl.edu/libphilprac/328*.

Porter, B. (2011) Millennial undergraduate research strategies in web and library information retrieval systems, *Journal of Web Librarianship* 5: 267–85.

Psaltou-Joycey, A. and Kantaridou, Z. (2011) Major, minor and negative learning style preferences of university students, *System* 39: 103–12.

Puchta, C. and Potter, J. (2004) *Focus Group Practice*. London: Sage Publications.

Rader, H.B. (2004) Building faculty–librarian partnerships to prepare students for information fluency, *C&RL News* (February): 74–6.

Ragains, P. (1997) Evaluation of academic librarians' instruction performance: report of a national survey, *Research Strategies* 15(3): 159–75.

Rainer, T.S. and Rainer, J. (2011) *The Millennials: Connecting to America's Largest Generation*. Nashville, TN: B&H Publishing Group.

Raspa, D. and Ward, D. (2000) *The Collaborative Imperative: Librarians and Faculty Working Together in the Information Universe*. Chicago, IL: American Library Association.

Ratteray, O.M.T. (2002) Information literacy in self-study and accreditation, *Journal of Academic Librarianship* 28(6): 368–75.

Rausch, J.L. and Hamilton, M.W. (2006) Goals and distractions: explanations of early attrition for traditional university freshmen, *Qualitative Report* 11(2): 317–34.

Reeves, R. and Hahn, T. (2010) A graduate degree in library or information science is required, but not sufficient, to enter the profession, *Journal of Education for Library and Information Science* 51(2): 103–19.

Robertson, A. and Smith, B. (1999) *Teaching in the 21st Century: Adapting Writing Pedagogies to the College Curriculum*. New York: Falmer Press.

Rockman, I.F. (2004) *Integrating Information Literacy into the Higher Education Curriculum: Practical Models for Transformation*. San Franscisco, CA: Jossey-Bass.

Rogers, K.M.A. (2009) A preliminary investigation and analysis of student learning preferences in further and higher education, *Journal of Further and Higher Education* 33(1): 13–21.

Roy, L. (2011) Library instruction: the teaching prong in the reference/readers' advisory/instruction triad, *The Reference Librarian* 52: 274–6.

Ruediger, C. and Jung, D. (2007) When it all comes together: integrating information literacy and discipline-based accreditation standards, *College & Undergraduate Libraries* 14(1): 79–87.

Ruediger, C. and Neal, S. (2004) Tapping into student networks. Butler Univesity, Digital Commons @ Butler University.

Sajdak, B.T. (2012) Let the faculty do it: responsibility and collaboration in developing an information literacy program, *College & Research Libraries News* 73(4): 196–9.

Salerno, C. (2012) Bitter reality of MOOConomics, *Inside HigherEd* (August). Available from: *http://www.inside highered.com/views/2012/08/09/real-economics-massive-online-courses-essay.*

Samson, S. and McCrea, D.E. (2008) Using peer review to foster good teaching, *Reference Services Review* 36(1): 61–70.

Sanderson, H. (2011) Using learning styles in information literacy: critical considerations for librarians, *Journal of Academic Librarianship* 37(5): 376–85.

Saunders, L. (2007) Regional accreditation organizations' treatment of information literacy: definitions, collaboration, and assessment, *Journal of Academic Librarianship* 33(3): 317–26.

Saunders, L. (2008) Perspectives on accreditation and information literacy as reflected in the literature of library and information science, *Journal of Academic Librarianship* 34(4): 305–13.

Saunders, L. (2012) Faculty perspectives on information literacy as a student learning outcome, *Journal of Academic Librarianship* 38(4): 226–36.

Selematsela, D.N.S. and du Toit, A.S.A. (2007) Competency profile for librarians teaching information literacy, *Journal of Librarianship and Information Science* 73(2): 297–300.

Selingo, J. (March 2012) The student swirl – next: Jeff Selingo's blog on rethinking higher education, *The Chronicle of Higher Education Online.* Available from: *http://chronicle.com/blogs/next/2012/03/08/the-student-swirl/.*

Shank, J.D. and Dewald, N.H. (2012) Academic library administrators' perceptions of four instruction skills, *College and Research Libraries* 73(1): 78–93.

Shell, L.B., Duvernay, J., Ewbank, A.D., Konomos, P., Leaming, A. et al. (2010) A comprehensive plan for library support of online and extended education, *Journal of Library Administration* 50: 951–71.

Shortland, S. (2004) Peer observation: a tool for staff development or compliance?, *Journal of Further and Higher Education* 28(2): 219–28.

Siddiqui, Z.S., Jonas-Dwyer, D. and Carr, S.E. (2007) Twelve tips for peer observation of teaching, *Medical Teacher* 29: 297–300.

Simmons, H.L. (1992) Information literacy and accreditation: a middle states association perspective, *New Directions for Higher Education* 78 (Summer): 15–25.

Simoneaux, S.L. and Stroud, C.L. (2011) SWOT analysis: the annual check-up for a business, *Journal of Pension Benefits* 18(3): 75–8.

Singer, P.M. and Griffith, G. (2010) *Succession Planning in the Library: Developing Leaders, Managing Change*. Chicago, IL: American Library Association.

Sokoloff, J. (2012) Information literacy in the workplace: employer expectations, *Journal of Business and Finance Librarianship* 17: 1–17.

Spooren, P., Mortelmans, D. and Denekens, J. (2007) Student evaluation of teaching quality in higher education: development of an instrument based on 10 Likert-scales, *Assessment & Evaluation in Higher Education* 32(6): 667–79.

Staines, G.M. (1990) Articulation agreements for bibliographic instruction, *Community & Junior College Libraries* 7(1): 17–26.

Stripling, B.K. and Hughes-Hassell, S. (2003) *Curriculum Connections through the Library*. Westport, CT: Libraries Unlimited.

Svinicki, M.D. and McKeachie, W.J. (2011) *McKeachie's Teaching Tips: Strategies, Research, and Theory for College and University Teachers*, 13th edition. Belmont, CA: Wadsworth/Cengage Learning.

Thrush, E.A. (2001) Plain English? A study of plain English vocabulary and international audiences, *Technical Communication* 48(3): 289–96.

Thull, J. (2008) Lifelong learning: libraries promote literacy throughout communities, *Tribal College Journal of American Indian Higher Education* 20(2): 26–9.

Tipton, R.L. and Bender, P. (2006) From failure to success: working with under-prepared transfer students, *Reference Services Review* 34(3): 389–404.

Tremblay, P. and Wang, Z. (2008) We care – virtually and in person: a user centered approach to assessment, implementation and promotion of library resources and services to a remote graduate campus, *Public Services Quarterly* 4(3): 207–32.

Tulgan, B. (6 June 2012) High-maintenance Generation Z heads to work, *USA Today*.

Twenge, J.M. (2006) *Generation Me: Why Today's Young Americans Are More Confident, Assertive, Entitled – and More Miserable than Ever Before*. New York: Free Press.

Tyron, J., Frigo, E. and O'Kelly, M. (2010) Using teaching faculty focus groups to assess information literacy core competencies at university level, *Journal of Information Literacy* 4(2): 62–77.

Van Cleave, K. (2007) Collaboration. In S.C. Curzon and L.D. Lampert (eds.), *Proven Strategies for Building an Information Literacy Program* (pp. 177–90). New York: Neal-Schulman Publishers.

Van Duinkerken, W. and Mosley, P.A. (2011) *The Challenge of Library Management: Leading with Emotional Engagement.* Chicago, IL: American Library Association.

Varner, C.H., Schwartz, V.M. and George, J. (1996) Library instruction and technology in a general education "gateway" course: the student's view, *Journal of Academic Librarianship* (September): 355–9.

Wallace, L.K. (2004) *Libraries, Mission, & Marketing: Writing Mission Statements That Work.* Chicago, IL: American Libraries Association.

Wallace, P. and Clariana, R.B. (2005) Perception versus reality – determining business students' computer literacy skills and need for instruction in information concepts and technology, *Journal of Information Technology Education* 4: 141–50.

Walter, S. (2008) Librarians as teachers: a qualitative inquiry into professional identity, *College & Research Libraries* 69(1): 51–71.

Warner, D.A. (2009) Programmatic assessment of information literacy skills using rubrics, *Journal on Excellence in College Teaching* 20(1): 149–64.

Warren, L.A. (2006) Information literacy in community colleges, *Reference and Users Services Quarterly* 45(4): 297–303.

Watstein, S.B., Wonsek, P.L. and Matthews, P. (1994) *Formal Planning in College Libraries.* Chicago, IL: American Libraries Association.

Weimer, M. and Lenze, L.F. (1997) Instructional interventions: a review of the literature on efforts to improve instruction. In J.C. Smart (ed.), *Higher Education: Handbook of Theory and Research*, Volume 7 (pp. 294–333). New York: Agathon Press.

Westbrock, T. and Fabian, S. (2010) Proficiencies for instruction librarians: is there still a disconnect between professional education and professional responsibilities? *College & Research Libraries* 71(6): 569–90.

Whitehurst, A. (2011) The assessment portfolio: a possible answer to the distance education assessment dilemma, *Internet Reference Services Quarterly* 16: 91–7.

Wright, M. and Grabowsky, A. (2011) The role of the adult educator in helping learners access and select quality health information on the Internet, *New Directions for Adult and Continuing Education* 130(Summer): 79–88.

Young, J.R. (2012) "Badges" earned online pose challenge to traditional college diplomas, *Chronicle of Higher Education* 58(19): A1–A4.

Zacharis, N.A. (2011) The effect of learning style on preference for web-based courses and learning outcomes, *British Journal of Educational Technology* 42(5): 790–800.

Zerihun, Z., Beishuizen, J. and Van Os, W. (2012) Student learning experience as indicator of teaching quality, *Educational Assessment Evaluation and Accountability* 24: 99–111.

Zmuda, A. (2007) Hitch your wagon to a mission statement, *School Library Media Activities Monthly* 24(1): 24–6.

Zoellner, K., Samson, S. and Hines, S. (2008) Continuing assessment of library instruction to undergraduates: a general education course survey research project, *College & Research Libraries* (July): 370–83.

Index

Lightning Source UK Ltd.
Milton Keynes UK
UKOW07f0018121214

242996UK00005B/41/P